A TREASURY OF INTERNATIONAL FOLK DANCES

A Step-by-Step Guide

Choreographed by

JIM GOLD

Full Court Press
Englewood Cliffs, New Jersey

First Edition

Copyright © 2019 by Jim Gold

Published in the United States of America
by Full Court Press, 601 Palisade Avenue,
Englewood Cliffs, NJ 07632
fullcourtpress.com

ISBN 978-1-946989-34-5
Library of Congress Catalog No. 2019908916

Editing and book design by Barry Sheinkopf

TO ALL MY FOLK DANCE TEACHERS

"I've traveled to many countries, seen many kinds of dances. All are true."
—Anonymous folk dance traveler

HOW TO USE THIS BOOK

1. Read the dance titles at the beginning of each entry.
2. Learn the dance name. Familiarize yourself with its background material.
3. Copy and paste the video link into your web browser and watch the dance. Or type the dance name into the YouTube search bar, followed by "Jim Gold folk dancer" (*Example: Kapura Jim Gold folk dancer,* or *Russian Round Jim Gold folk dancer,* or *El Pastor Jim Gold folk dancer*). Hit *Enter.*
4. As you watch, practice the steps using the video to guide you.
5. After that, read the written instructions for a more exact understanding of the steps, rhythms, and other details of the dance
6. Finally—and primarily—enjoy the dance!

ABOUT THE AUTHOR

JIM GOLD BRINGS A LOVE of people, music, languages, humor, old cultures, and new discoveries to his life's work. His adventures as an author, musician, folk dance teacher, tour leader, and entrepreneur make his programs a joy for people of all ages. He is a dance teacher who makes it easy.

After graduating from the High School of Music and Art in New York City, he studied violin at the Eastman School of Music, and spent a year at the University of Aix-en-Provence in Southern France. Then he returned to the University of Chicago for a B.A. in history, and later, an M.A. in music from New York University.

A classical and folk guitarist, Mr. Gold's *World of Guitar* concert program has appeared in schools, colleges, and community concerts throughout the United States. He founded the classic guitar department at Montclair State University, performed on radio, television, and has recorded three classical and folk guitar records. He is also the author of eight books. He heads his own company (Jim Gold International), teaches folk dance classes, and organizes folk music and dance weekends.

Through his Jim Gold Tours, he leads travel groups to exotic countries such as Bulgaria, Hungary, Spain, Romania, Turkey, Croatia, and Tunisia to experience history, culture, and folklore. Jim is an avid student of languages, yoga, running, history, the Bulgarian bagpipe (gaida), and mysteries of the human mind.

PREFACE

CHOREOGRAPHIES ARE CREATED in the imagination and dreams of choreographers. If steps do not exist, or have yet to be created, the choreographer begins to move. Soon a dance appears.

A folk dance choreographer is steeped in lore, folk dance music, culture, history, art, steps, and national style. The steps he or she creates are faithful to the dancing style of the native country.

But no matter what the choreographer creates, choreographies are really suggested steps. All dances are open to interpretation and subject to future improvisations depending on the imagination, ingenuity, and creativity of the teacher or leader presenting them. And this whether created in a village, a native country, or the new world.

The relatively new art form of international folk dancing is developing and growing in the United States and throughout the world. Along with more traditional approaches, new bands have also formed. The new music they create is often based on a fusion of folk traditions and modern styles. With so many beautiful songs, striking harmonies, and tingling vibrations presently nourishing your mind, what else can you do but dance?

Join the creative stream! Become part of this flow!

I will consider this book a success if it inspires other folk dance teachers, leaders, and dancers to follow their inner muse and create exciting new dance steps, as I have done, in the folk tradition.

When I was twenty-four years old, I worked as a waiter in a hotel in New York's Adirondack Mountains. Until then, I had never danced. One night, I peeked into a folk dance evening that Fritzi Gerber was leading. She was dressed in a folk dance outfit and made quite a picture. There were about a hundred people in the room, noisily milling about. Suddenly, she moved to the middle of the room, raised her hand, and in about five seconds, the room became totally quiet and still. I was shocked and amazed. What had this woman just done? How did she have this power to so quickly silence such an unruly mob? Then Fritzi told everyone to form a circle, and she began teaching her first dance (which I believe was "Ersko Kolo," from Serbia).

I also stepped into the circle. At the end of the class, Fritzi said she was teaching folk dancing every afternoon in the clubhouse at the edge of the lake. I decided to give it a try. After I finished waiting tables at lunch, I went down to the lake. Fritzi taught "Sestorka" (also from Serbia). It was the first dance I ever learned. I had never heard such exciting and beautiful music before. I ended up totally thrilled. That afternoon class began a process that changed my life.

After that summer of folk dancing, I returned to my apartment in New York's Greenwich Village. I searched out folk dancing and found all kinds everywhere. I started going to classes. Coming from a formal classical music background (I played violin and, later, clasical guitar), I just loved the informality of the folk dance scene and its acceptance of almost anyone who tried to dance, no matter how unskilled or timid they were. Plus, the music was so beautiful and exciting! I couldn't resist.

So three or four times a week, I went dancing wherever I could find it—Polish, Ukrainian, Israeli, international, whatever. I loved the music, and I loved to improvise. This was also true when I improvised while dancing the "Hambo" at International House in New York, and the teacher, Marianne Hermann, threw me off the dance floor, because I was going in the wrong direction, knocking off people and couples as we moved in opposite directions around the room! I remember wondering why she would bother doing that. After all, I was just making up steps and not bothering or hurting anyone, and careful not to bump into others as I and my partner traveled in reverse around the room. But stop me she did. That was my first public attempt at improvising.

Several years earlier, I had given up violin and learned how to play guitar and sing folk songs. I also started taking classical and flamenco guitar lessons. (Teaching, and giving concerts, on classical and folk guitar later became my career for about fifteen years.) I also played guitar for an Israeli folk dance performing group called Aviv. (Peter Yarrow later took my place.) Its lead dancer was Sonny Newman. When Aviv disbanded, Sonny decided to open a folk dance studio on Twenty-third Street in Manhattan. This second-floor studio soon became a Mecca for excited new folk dancers. I learned many folk dances at Sonny's.

At the time, I also worked as a social director in a Catskill Mountain Hotel called Chaits. One of my duties was teaching folk dancing. By then, I knew about ten dances and taught them all. Although I didn't realize it at the time, that summer was the beginning of my teaching career. After I got married, my wife and I decided to buy a house and moved from Greenwich Village to Teaneck, New Jersey. The only class I knew of around Teaneck and in the North Jersey area was one given in nearby Hackensack by Ken Spear. My wife and I went to his class, but as it happened Kenny was sick that night, and the class was cancelled. Then one of the dancers said to me, "Hey, Jim, you taught dancing this summer, and you've got some records at home. Why not go get them and bring them down, so we can dance?" I agreed. I went home, got the records, and ran the class. Soon after that, Ken Spear decided to give it up, and I was elected to take it over.

After a year of teaching, I realized I didn't know very much. Then a pivotal event took place. I went dancing at Fourteenth Street in New York. A new teacher named Kalman Magyar, from Hungary, came to the class. He told the class about the new Hungarian dance class he was starting at Hungary House uptown, and he took one leap to demonstrate a dance. I said, "Wow! I want to leap like that. And I want to dance like that!" So I attended his first classes.

Kalman had a teaching method I just loved. He would put on Hungarian music, stand in front of the class, and improvise steps. He'd do it for two hours. He'd start easy, look around the room to see if everyone was getting the steps, then add a more advanced movement, always checking the room to see how people were doing. If they got it, he'd stay with the advanced steps; if not, he'd return to something simpler until the people got that, then slowly move back to the advanced, always improvising, always watching. And in all this time he hardly said a word. I dubbed this the "Hungarian teaching method." And it, based on improvisation, was (and remains) the method I eventually adopted and developed to teach my own folk dance classes.

After I had given up my class in Hackensack and after a couple of years dancing Hungarian dancing with Kalman, there were still no folk dance classes in Teaneck. I started a group with three other teachers;

we each taught for one week a month. The three others soon quit, but I decided to continue. Although I was still earning my living by giving concerts, that was the true beginning of my folk dance teaching "career."

In 1982, someone suggested that, since I had experience in Catskill Mountain hotels working as a social director, I organize and run a folk dance weekend. I agreed, did it, and about a hundred people attended! I was shocked and amazed to realize I could potentially make a living out of this! Imagine! I already had experience making a living out of another "impossible" business, concertizing as a classical and folk guitarist. I thought, Why not? I was ready for a new career anyway; why not give folk dancing a try? In the beginning, I could simply add it to my guitar concerts. The rest is history.

WHEN I STARTED TEACHING folk dancing, and creating my own interpretations of the music, making up my own steps, people told me the steps were wrong!

I wondered how they knew?

Was there a "correct" Bulgarian step? A "correct" Polish, French, Hungarian, Greek, Albanian, Croatian, Serbian, Turkish, Israeli, etc. step? Did people in these countries only dance one way?

I belonged then to the group taught by Kalman Magyar, whose teaching "method" was to improvise, making up steps to Hungarian folk music as he went along. It was, as I have said, deeply exciting and inspiring.

I loved it. I wanted to teach that way also, but didn't know exactly how to go about it.

My main question remained: Did people in these countries really dance? In villages, weddings, parties, social gathering, wherever people danced, did they actually perform the steps we learned in folk dance classes?

And if they did, how?

The best way to find out was to go these countries and see for myself.

Although I knew I could always do that, I also knew that most folk dance groups in these countries would much rather meet me if I brought along a group of Americans.

So in 1984, with the help of Kalman, I decided to organized my first folk dance tour to Hungary.

Five years earlier, Karl Finger, along with Yves Moreau, had organized a tour to Bulgaria, the first dance tour of its kind. I was good friends with Karl, so my wife Bernice and I decided to go. We visited the town of Dospat, located high in the Rhodope Mountains. We had learned "Dospatsko Horo" in America and wanted to show the villagers that we could dance it. When we arrived in Dospat, our group got out of the bus, entered the village square, and, as all the local Bulgarian stood around, watching in amazement, we danced "Dospatsko Horo." But to my surprise, although the Bulgarians knew the music, they didn't know—and had never seen—this dance!

This was a powerful moment, the first time I realized that international folk dancers did indeed do things "differently." That meant there were no "right" steps!

Slowly a purpose formed in my mind. I decided to travel to countries whose dances I loved. I would find out first hand (or first foot) how the folks there actually folk danced. My plan soon grew to include all the countries of Europe and the Middle East. By adding one new county a year, I would eventually reach my goal.

Before touring each country, I spent a year studying its language, culture, history, and traditions.

My first year was my Hungarian year. Before organizing and leading the trip, I spent the year taking Hungarian language lessons, and studying every history, geography, and traditions book (in English) that I could find.

The second year is was Russian. I followed the same method, then ran a trip to what was then the Soviet Union. I was determined to educate myself and immerse myself in the styles and traditions of those countries in order to know and feel comfortable with the technique of improvising and choreographing dances. And I in fact added a new country each year.

I had been a "closet choreographer" for years. When I taught a dance I had choreographed, I never told anyone. I was afraid that, if they knew, they would (immediately) reject it as "inauthentic."

In 2004 Lee Otterholt and I were invited

to teach at Florida Folk Dance Camp. Lee is not only a Norwegian and Balkan dance expert, but a choreographer! That's when I "admitted" to him that I had choreographed many dances.

To my happy surprise, he said, "Why, that's great!" He gave me the confidence to start admitting it and going public.

Then I started asking other teachers if they choreographed, too. It turned out many of them did. But they too had hesitated and been afraid to say so, fearing the international folk dance community, the folk dance public, would think their dances "inauthentic."

But what is folk dancing but "folks dancing." The teachers all wanted to teach "authentic" dances (what "folks" in these foreign countries danced). But when villagers from other countries dance at special events, they usually dance only one step. And they may dance the same step for hours! At a wedding, party, or festival, with food, lots of friends, and live music, some might do a variation or two, others might dance a few minutes, drop out, chat, then rejoin the circle to dance some more. How exciting were these "simple" events–for the villagers and locals, one step was often enough.

International folk dance classes lack this atmosphere. Since there is no food, wedding, party, festival, or whatever, folk dance teachers often add new steps (improvise and choreograph) to make the experience more interesting. Without them, the dancers might get bored and go home. And since teachers want to make a living, they want to please their customers (dancers), so they make up steps, add steps, to hold their audience. Very normal and natural in order to survive.

Leading tours, seeing how people in these countries dance, has taught me how to simplify dances down to their basic elements. I make them so simple anyone can do them! (Simplicity, accessibility—that's what I consider to be the true folk style

But by leading tours, my travelers and I see people from these countries actually dancing their folk dances! And yes, the locals may add a variation or two. This helps remind me that it's okay to improvise, to create "on the spot."

I feel choreography is necessary and important, first, because creating is part of being human, and choreography is part of being human. It can't be stopped. Nor should it be. Choreography is an inner necessity. It allows for freedom, breaks boundaries, and depending on how daring we are, takes us places and on adventures we never imagined existed.

And, of course, I don't want the dancers to be bored. As you know, stage performances are always choreographed to make them interesting for the audience, but the original steps somewhere in there. I use the traditional forms but change some things.

There is, moreover, no one grand and

unified folk dance community, only small ones. Each has its own life. These different "villages" do the steps they want to make themselves, and their audience happy. Period.

You don't feel you are "changing" "folk" dances?

There are many traditions people love and want to keep; but a Heraclitus said, fire is the origin of all things, permanence an illusion, for everything is in a process of constant change.

He also said that you can't step in the same river twice and, if he'd been asked, would probably have added that you can't put your foot in the same dance twice. Change in folk dancing and choreography, as in every other pursuit, is the nature of life.

To my surprise, most people, if they this approach to dance, say, "Wow!" Then maybe later, they might ask, "How do you do it?"

Perhaps the word "choreograph" has too many syllables and is too elaborate a word. Maybe "create" would be better.

I have choreographed about two hundred folk dances. This volume contains notations for the greater part of them.

ABBREVIATIONS

bkwd: Backward

ct: Count, in the musical measure of a dance

ctr: Center

CW: Clockwise

CCW: Counter clockwise

diag: diagonal

dir: direction

ft: Foot

fwd: Fwd

LOD: Line of Direction—refers to the direction
of the dance, usually right or left

L: Left

opp: opposite

R: Right

x: times

GLOSSARY

Alunelul Step: From the Romanian name for hazelnut tree, whose branches
have magical properties—including water divination. Named after the
Romanian dance Alunelul.

Belt Hold: Dancers hold belts or sashes. Often used in Balkan dances.

Csardas: National dance of Hungary. Usually done as a couple dance but
sometimes danced in improvised form in a circle or line. Coming from
csarda, the Hungarian word for tavern, a place where peasants,
farmers, and local townspeople met to dance a couple dance with a
simple side-together-side step. After the revolution of 1848, it became
the national dance.

Cherkessia: The name means Caucasus. Based on name and crossing step
of Circassian people from Caucasia, the Caucasus region.

Clogging: Tap dance step from the southern Appalachians. Originally
from Ireland and the British Isles.

Drmes: Trembling step from Croatia where it is danced in a circle. Etymologically, *drmes* is related to Turkish name *dervish* and thus to the whirling dervish dance itself. *Drmes* and *dervish* are also related to the Indo-Iranian root word for door. When one dances the Turkish meditative whirling dervish dance, or the circular Croatian *drmes*, one opens the door to heaven.

Escort Position: Dancer places hand on hip; adjacent dancer takes his or her arm by the elbow.

Grapevine: Lateral twisting step: the fastest, easiest way to move sideward.

Hasapico: Greek butcher's dance. From Turkish *hasap*, butcher. Slow, heavy, sensual, inward, and meditative in mode and feeling. Originally, dance of the Greek butcher's guild in Constantinople during the twelfth century.

Hornpipe Step: Rocking step simulating a sailor's first unsteady steps on land, before they get their "land legs."

Klezmer: From Hebrew *Kli'zemer*. *Kli* means vessel, pot, or musical instrument. *Zemer* means song. Jewish dance style from Eastern Europe based on local and national dance forms.

Kopanitsa: From kopan, to dig. A lively Bulgarian folk dance in $^{11}/_{16}$ timing.

Lame Duck step: Hopping type step from Croatia.

Pas de Bas: Leap and crossing step. Shortened form of *pas de Basque*, "step of the Basques."

Pontozo: Hungarian word for "point," as in the point or period ending a sentence. Virtuoso men's dance from Transylvania filled with twists, slaps, and leaps.

Pravo Horo: The lively, spirited national dance of Bulgaria. Related to the Russian *pravda*, "truth" or "right." Typical three-measure hora or horo dance pattern.

Ragtime csardas: *Csardas* step danced to ragtime music.

Rida: Crossing step.

Ronde de Jambe: From French "circling round of the leg." Lift leg with thigh parallel to floor; then trace a circle in the air with your leg.

Ruchenitza: A Bulgarian folk dance in $^{7}/_{16}$ time. Danced solo, in couples, or in a line. Etymologically, related to reka, hand, or retchenik, handkerchief often waved or rotated by the dance leader.

Schottishe: Derives from Scottish. Walk and hop step danced in northern Europe.

Shirto, or Syrto: Syrto is the Greek national dance, a four-measure, open - circle dance in ⅞ time, originating in the Peloponnesian town of Kalamata—famous for its olives. Syrto is often called Kalamatianos. Also danced in Western Bulgaria where it is called Shirtos.

Shoulder Hold: Dancers hold shoulders of neighboring dancers.

Suzie Q: Twisting, pigeon-toed, sidewards step, often danced in Ragtime dancing.

Shuffle: Clogging step.

Simian Gallop: Dancing like a gorilla.

Tarantella: Popular improvised dance from South Italy and Sicily in lively ⅝ time (sometimes ¾) Some claim the dance is named after the Southern Italian town of Tarentum, and relates to the movements off, or bites from, the Tarantula spider.

Two-step: Two quick steps followed by one slow step, danced moving forward or in place. Also called *pas de bas*, Serbian two-step, Yemenite step, Texas two-step, and more.

V position: Dancers holding hands, arms at sides, making shape of a "V."

W position: Dancers hold hands, arms held at shoulder height, forming shape of a "W."

TABLE OF CONTENTS

Á LA CLAIRE FONTAINE (France)

Dance Meaning: By the Clear Fountain
Choreography: By Jim Gold in international folk dance style
Music: Nana Mouskouri
Formation: Open circle, hands in V position
Meter: 2/4
YouTube video link: *http://bit.ly/2lH5xO0*

> **Introduction:** 8 meas Meas 5-8: Holding step: Place R toe next to L facing diag CCW

Measures

FIRST STEP

Moving CCW
Two-steps, crossing step, sway

1	Step R (ct 1), bring L to R (ct &) step R (ct 2)
2	Step L (ct 1, bring R next to L (ct &), step L (ct 2)

Crossing step

3	Step R front of L (ct 1), step back on L (ct 2)
4	Step back on R (ct 1), step on L in place (ct 2)
5-8	Repeat meas 1-4
9	Sway rt (ct 1), sway lft (ct 2), lift R (ct 3)

SECOND STEP

Moving CW
4-step grapevine, two 2-steps, 1 crossing step, tch

1	Cross R over L (ct 1), step L to lft (ct 2)
2	Step R behind L (ct 1), step L to lft (ct 2)

Two 2-steps CW

3	Step R across L (ct 1), bring L behind R (ct &), step R (ct 2)
4	Step L to lft (ct 1), step R behind L (ct &), step L (ct 2)

Crossing step

5	Cross R over L, bringing L ft behind rt calve (ct 1), step back on L (ct 2)

Holding step

6	Tch R toe next to L facing diag rt CCW (ct 1-2)

ORDER OF STEPS
1. First Step: 1x, Second Step: 1x
Ending: Dance Second Step meas 1-5, then repeat entire Second Step

A La Claire Fontaine

A la claire fontaine
M'en allant promener
J'ai trouve l'eau si belle
Que je m'y suis baigne

Il y a longtemps que je t'aime
Jamais je ne t'oublierai

Sous les feuilles de chene
Je me suis fait seche
Sur la plus haute branche
Le rossignol chantait

Il y a longtemps que je t'aime
Jamais je ne t'oublierai

Chante, rossignol, chante
Toi qui as le coeur gai
Tu as le coeur rire
Moi je l'ai pleurer

Il y a longtemps que je t'aime
Jamais je ne t'oublierai

C'est pour mon ami Pierre
Qui ne veut plus m'aimer
Pour un bouton de rose
Que je lui refusai

Il y a longtemps que je t'aime
Jamais je ne t'oublierai

J'ai perdu mon ami
Sans l'avoir merite
Pour un bouquet de roses
Que je lui refusai

Il y a longtemps que je t'aime
Jamais je ne t'oublierai

AIDE, ODAM, ODAM (BULGARIA)

Dance Meaning: Come (Let's go), I go, Odam
Pronunciation: Aide, Odam, Odam
Choreography: By Jim Gold in Bulgarian folk dance style
Music: Zdravko Georgev
Formation: Open Circle, arms in W position
Meter: 7/8: slow/quick/quick: s, q, q
Jim Gold YouTube video: *https://www.youtube.com/watch?v=SpzTRb1bXAM*
Introduction: 8 measures
Measures:

FIRST STEP
Face and move CCW, two-step and crossing step
1   Face rt, step on R (s), step fwd on L (q), step fwd on R (q)
2   Repeat meas 1 opp ft
3   Face ctr, step on R in place, cross L over R (q)
        Step on R in place (q)
4   Repeat meas 3 opp ft
5-12   Repeat meas 1-4 2x
13-15   Repeat meas 1-3
16   Step on L in place(s), tch rt toe next to L heel (q, q)

SECOND STEP
Lesnoto, hold, and turn
1   Face ctr, step to rt on R (s), lift L (q), cross L over R (q)
2   Step on R and lift L (s), bounce on R (q), bounce on R (q)
3   Repeat meas 2 opp ft
4   Face ctr, step to rt on R (s), lift L (q), cross L over R (q)
5   Step on R and slowly lift L (s, q, q)
        Hold lifted L, slow double bounce on R
6   Bounce on R (s), bounce on R(q, q)
7   Step fwd on L (s, q, q)
8   Tch R heel fwd (s), tch R heel diag to rt (q, q)
9-16   Repeat meas 1-8
17-23   Repeat meas 1-7
        Full CCW turn
24   Step fwd on L, pivot CCW (s)
        Step on R in place facing ctr (q), step on L in place (q)

ORDER OF STEPS
1. First Step: 1x, Second Step: 1x

AJ DA IDEM JANO (BULGARIA)

Dance Meaning: Let' Go Jano
Pronunciation: Aye Da Eedem Yano
Choreography: By Jim Gold in Bulgarian folk dance style. April/2013
Music: Unknown
Formation: Open circle
Meter: 4/4
Jim Gold YouTube video: *http://bit.ly/2lBOLyI*
Introduction: 6 measures
Measures

FIRST STEP
Face ctr. Sides, fwd and back

1   Step R to rt (ct 1), step L behind R (ct 2)
       Step R (ct 3), Lift L (ct 4

2   Repeat meas 1 opp dir, opp ft
       Into ctr

3   Step R fwd (ct 1), step L fwd (ct 2)
       step R fwd (ct 3), lift L (ct 4)
       Moving back

4   Step back on L (ct 1), back on R (ct 2)
       Back on L (ct 3), tch L next to R (ct 4)

5-8   Repeat meas 1-4

SECOND STEP
Moving LOD, CCW: Grapevine and 2 lifts

1   Step R to rt (ct 1), cross L front of R and dip (ct 2)
       Step R to rt (ct 3), step L behind R (ct 4)

2   Step R (ct 1), lift L (ct 2), step L (ct 3), lift R (ct 4)

ORDER OF STEPS
1. First Step: 2x, Second Step: 8x

AKO OOMRA (BULGARIA)

Dance Meaning: If I Die
Pronunciation: A-ko OO-mra
Choreography: By Jim Gold in Bulgarian folk dance style
Style: Pirin Region, Shirto, arms in W hold, West Bulgarian folk dance style
Music: Peroun: Posloushaite Patrioti. Ako Oomra
Formation: Open circle, arms in W position.
Meter: 7/8 slow/quick/quick: s, q, q
Jim Gold YouTube video: *http://bit.ly/2lEpgMW*
Introduction: 10 measures
Measures:

FIRST STEP
Shirtos
1   Walk to right, CCW: Lift and slight hesitation on first step (beat)
     Arms W position: R (s), L (q), R (q)
2   L (s), R (q), L (q)
     Moving out of circle, bring arms down
3   R (s), L (q), R (q)
     In place, bring arms up
4   L (s), cross R over L (q), step on L in place (q).
5-16 Repeat measures 1-4 3x

SECOND STEP (A)
Walk into ctr
1   R (s), L (q), R (q)
2   L (s), R (q), L (q)
3   Step to right on R (s), step L behind R (q, q)
4   Step to right on R (s), lift L (q, q)
5   Walk bkwd: L (s), R (q),L (q)
6   R (s), L (q), R (q),
7   Step to left on L (s), step R behind L (q, q)
8   Step to left on L (s), lift R (q, q)
9   2 back pas de bas: step to right on R (s)
     Step on L behind (q), step on R in place (q)
10   Repeat meas 9 opp dir., opp ft

SECOND STEP (B)
Walk into ctr
1   R (s), L (q), R (q)
2   L (s), R (q), L (q)
3   Step to right on R (s), step in L behind R (q, q)
4   Step to right on R (s), lift L (q, q)
5   Walk bkwd: L (s), R (q), L (q)
6   R (s), L (q), R (q)
7   Step to left on L (s), step on R behind L (q, q)
8   Step to left on L(s), touch R to L instep (q, q)

ORDER OF STEPS
1. First Step: 4x, Second Step: A:1x, B: 1x

AL ALEM ALLAH (Egypt)

Dance Meaning: God Only Knows
Pronunciation: Al Alem Allah
Choreography: By Jim Gold in Arab Debka folk dance style
Music: Amr Diab: Tamally Maak from Egypt
Formation: Line
Meter: 2/4
Jim Gold YouTube video: *https://www.youtube.com/watch?v=f7B7vXjkpaA*
Introduction: 8 measures
Measures:

FIRST STEP
    Debka Step 4x
    Debka walk, moving CCW, hands in V position

1	Tch L heel to floor (ct 1) , step on full L ft (ct 2)
2	Tch R heel to floor (ct 1) , step on full R ft (ct 2)
3-4	Repeat meas 1-2
5	Tch L toe fwd (ct 1)
6	Tch L toe to lft side (ct 2)
7-24	Repeat meas 1-6 3x
25	**Ending:** Step on L in place (ct 1-2)
26	Stamp on R next to L (ct 1- 2)

SECOND STEP   (9 meas plus 8 meas)
    Two Arabic "rida" steps, hands in W position

1	Step R to Rt (ct 1), cross L in front of R (ct 2)
2	Repeat meas 1 (ct 1-2)
	Rocking step
3	Step back on R (ct 1), step fwd on L (ct 2)
4	Brush R fwd (ct 1), step fwd on R (ct 2)
	2 Steps fwd
5	Step fwd on L (ct 1), big step fwd on R (ct 2)
	Double bounce step
6	Face slight leftward: quarter-squat (ct 1)
	Double bounce in place (ct 2, ct &)
7	Repeat meas 6
	Walk back 4 steps
8	R (ct 1), L (ct 2)
9	R (ct 3), L (ct 4)

10-17 Repeat meas 1-17
18   Walk back two steps: R (ct 1), L (ct 2).

THIRD STEP
Hands in W position
1   Sway rt on R (ct 1), sway lft on L (ct 2,
2   Cross R over L (ct 1), tch L to left side (ct 2)
3   Step fwd (into ctr) on L (ct 1), **twist step:** tch R toe (ct 2), tch R heel (ct &)
4   Step back on R (ct 1), step on L in place next to R (ct 2)
5-12   Repeat above step 2x
13-15 Repeat meas 1-3 2x
16   Step back on R (ct 1), **stamp on L** next to R (ct 1-2)

ORDER OF STEPS
1.   First Step: 4x , Second Step: 2x. Third Step: 4x
       First Step: 4x, Second Step: 2x, Third step: 4x
       First Step: 4x, Second Step: 2x, Third step: 4x

       Third Step: 2x, First Step: (4x)
       Walk fwd in LOD:
1-2   L (ct 1), R (ct 2), L (ct 1), Step on R in place (ct 2)
       Wait during 4 drums beats (ct 1-2,4x)

INTERLUDE
Arabian Side-Together
1   Step to R (ct 1-2)
2   Bring L next to R (ct1- 2)
3   Step to L (ct 1-2)
4   Bring R next to L (ct 1-2)
5-8   Repeat meas 1-4
Arabian Double Time
1   Step to R (ct 1), bring L next to R (ct 2)
2   Step to L (ct 1), bring R next to L (ct 2)
3   Step to R (ct 1), bring L next to R (ct &)
4   Step to L (ct 2), bring R next to L (ct &)
5-8   Repeat meas 1-4

       Third Step: 4x
       Second Step: 2x

Ending: Walk back 5 steps:

1   R (ct 1), L(ct 2)
2   R (ct 1), L (ct 2)
3   Walk back one step R (ct 1)
     Tch L heel in place, raise rt hand high, hold(ct 2)

ALE BRIDER (YIDDISH)

Dance Meaning: All Brothers
Pronunciation: AL-a BREED-der
Choreography: By Jim Gold in Klezmer folk dance style
Style: Eastern European/Klezmer dance style
Music: Itzak Perlman and the Klezmatics
Formation: Open circle, arms in W position
Meter: 2/4
Jim Gold YouTube video: *http://bit.ly/2mNoKOi*
Introduction: 4 measures
Measures:

FIRST STEP: Moving CCW: Arms pushing forward and back

1	Step to right on R, arms push straight forward (ct 1)
	Step L behind R, bringing arms back to shoulder height (ct 2)
2-7	Repeat measure 1 7x
8	Step on R (ct 1), lift L high to L while leaning to the right
9-13	Repeat meas 1 opp ft in opp dir 5x
14	Step on L (ct 1), kick R forward (ct 2)

Gypsy turn

15-16	Place right heel to left of L ft, turn clockwise in 1 ½ measures (ct 1, 2, 1)
	Bring R ft next to L ft (ct 2)

SECOND STEP

Forward into ctr of circle

1-2	R (ct 1), L (ct 2), R (ct 1), touch L forward (ct 2)
3	Bkwd out of circle: L (ct 1), R (ct 2)
4	In place: L (ct 1), R (ct &), L (ct 2)
5-6	Repeat meas 1-2
7	Repeat meas 3
8	Place L ft next to R (ct 1), heel stand: both ft together dip back on heels (ct 2)

3 grapevine steps to the left, CW

9	Step on R in front of L (ct 1), step on L to left side of R (ct 2)
10	Step on R behind L (ct 1, step L to left side of R (ct 2)
11-12	Repeat meas 9-10
13-14	Repeat meas 9-10

3 stamps

15-16	Stamp on R ft diag out (ct 1), stamp toward ctr of circle (ct 2)
	Stamp diag out (ct 1 and 2)

ALLA MIA FORA (Greece)

Dance Meaning: One more time, once again—("Alla": other or another, "Mia" a or one, "Fora": Time)

Choreography: By Jim Gold in Greek folk dance style

Music: Kauyta Laika 2012

Formation: Line

Meter: 2/4

Jim Gold YouTube video: *https://www.youtube.com/watch?v=2-ZclY_EFM0*

Introduction: 8 measures, then meas 5-8 of SECOND STEP (syrtos)

Measures:

FIRST STEP

Into ctr. Style: Heavy, stagger

1 Step fwd on R slight diag "stagger" (ct 1), fwd on L (ct 2)

2 Step fwd on R (ct 1), step L next to R (ct &), step fwd on R (ct 2)

3 Step fwd on L (ct 1), step R next to L (ct 2), step fwd on L next to R (ct &)

Tch R heel 2x (Optional: Tch toe, as in video)

4 Tch R toe fwd (ct 1), repeat tch R heel (ct 2)

5 Step back on R (ct 1), step back on L (ct 2)

6 Step R to rt (ct 1), lift L behind R (ct 2)

Move CW

7 Step L to lft (ct 1), cross R over L (ct 2)

8 Step L to lft (ct 1), close L to R , no weight (ct 2)

SECOND STEP

2/4 Syrtos

Face ctr, moving CCW

1 Step to R (ct 1), step L behind R (ct 2), step R to rt (ct &)

2 Face CCW: Hop on R, step on L (ct 1), step fwd R (ct 2), step fwd on L (ct &)

3 Step R in place (ct 1), step L in front (ct 2) , step R in place (ct &)

4 Step back on L (ct 1), step back on R (ct 2), step on L in place (ct &)

5 Face ctr: Step to R (ct 1), step L behind R(ct 2), step R to rt (ct &)

6 Face CCW: Hop on R, step on L (ct 1), step fwd R (ct 2)
   step fwd on L (ct &)

7 Face ctr: Step R to rt (ct 1), close L to R (ct 2)

8 Step L to lft (ct 1), lift R behind L (ct 2)

ORDER OF STEPS

1. First Step: 2x, Second Step: 2x

AM O MANDRA (ROMANIA)

Dance Meaning: I Have A Girl (Maiden)
Pronunciation: Am O MUN-dra
Choreography: By Jim Gold in Romanian dance style
Music: Bijuterii Folclorice: Moldova
Formation: Line. Arms in V position.
Meter: 4/4
YouTube video link: *https://www.youtube.com/watch?v=tUMv9N9no1Y*
Youteube Teaneck Seniors: https://www.youtube.com/watch?v=2f5AijXI3LI
Introduction: 8 measures
Measures:

FIRST STEP
Facing ctr, Romanian csardas step

1 Step to right on R (ct 1), bring L next to R (ct 2)
   Step to right on R (ct 3), touch L next to R (ct 4)

2 Step to left on L (ct 1), bring R next to L (ct 2)
   Step to left on L (ct 3), touch R next to L (ct 4)

3 Step fwd on R (ct 1)
   Lift on R, bring L ft behind R knee (ct 2)
   Step back on L (ct 3), step on R next to L (ct &)
   Step on L in place (ct 4)

4 Repeat meas 3
   Syncopated step

5 Step on R (ct 1), tap L heel next to R (ct &),
   Lift L (ct 2), tap L next to R (ct &),
   Step on L (ct 1), tap R heel next to L (ct &),
   Lift R (ct 2), tap R next to L (ct &).

6 Repeat meas 5

7-8 Repeat meas 3-4

9-10 Repeat meas 5-6

SECOND STEP
Moving to the right, CCW

1 Leap diagonally right on R (ct 1), leap diagonally left on L (ct 2)
   Moving straight LOD
   Step fwd on R (ct 3), bring L next to R (ct &), step fwd on R (ct 4)

2 Repeat meas 1 with opp ft

3-4 Repeat meas 1-2

Face ctr, 7 side-behind steps to right, CCW

5   Step to right on R (ct 1), step L behind R (ct 2)
     step to right on R (ct 3), step L behind R (ct 4)

6   Step to right on R (ct 1), step L behind R (ct 2)
     Step to right on R (ct 3), stamp on L (ct 4)

7   Repeat meas 5 opp dir with opp ft

8   Step to left on L (ct 1), step R behind L (ct 2)
     step to left on L (ct 3), lift on R, twist R leg to left, half turn, face left,
     CW (ct 4)

9-12 Repeat meas 1-4

Face ctr, 7 crossing steps moving left, CW

13   Cross R in front of L (ct 1) bring L next to R (ct 2)
     Cross R in front of L (ct 3), bring L next to R (ct 4)

14   Cross R in front of L (ct 1), bring L next to R (ct 2)
     Cross R in front of L (ct 3), lift high on L preparing
     to change directions (ct 4),

7 crossing step to right, CCW

15   Cross L in front of R (ct 1), bring R next to L (ct 2)
     Cross L in front of R (ct 3), bring R next to L (ct 4)

16   Cross L in front of R (ct 1), bring R next to L (ct 2)
     Cross L front of R (ct 3)
     Lift R, place behind L knee, half turn, face right, CCW (ct 4)

17-18 Repeat meas 1-2

19-20 Repeat meas 1-2 of First Step

B MORETO LODKA IS RATEVKA (Bulgaria)

Dance Meaning: Boat on the water

Pronunciation: V mo-RE-to LOT-ka

Choreography: By Jim Gold in Bulgarian folk dance style. Use as preliminary teaching dance for Ratevka. Choreography is same as Ratevka but slow, easy, lesnoto style. Follow B Moreto Lodka by dancing the original (faster) Ratevka.

Source: Pirin Region, West Bulgaria

Music: Posloushaite Patrioti, Peroun

Formation: Open Circle, hands down, arms in V position.

Meter: 7/8 slow/quick/quick s, q, q (or q, qq, qq)

YouTube video (Jim Gold dancing): *http://bit.ly/2oP41Lc*

Introduction: 4 measures

Measures:

FIRST STEP
4 Walking steps to right, CCW

1   R (s), L (q, q)

2   R (s), L (q,), quickly leap onto R (q)

3   Continuing CCW: step on L (s) , step to right (q), step on L behind R (q)

4   Step on R in place (s), cross L over R (q) , step back on R (q)

5   Step on L (s), lift R and in large reel step moving it bkwd (q) step on R in back of (q)

6   Step on L (s), lift and hold R (q, q)

7   Back out of circle: Step back on R (s), back on L (q), back on R (q)

8   Step on L in place (s), lift and hold R(q, q)

BATUTA DE LA SAUCHESHTI (Moldavia)

Dance meaning: Batuta from Saucheshti "Batuta" is a generic name of a Romanian dance with 0light stamping steps . Saucesti is a village in Moldavia.

Choreography: By Jim Gold in Romanian folk dance style

Music: Steve Kotansky's collection

Formation: Line, arms in W position

Meter: 2/4

Jim Gold YouTube video: *https://www.youtube.com/watch?v=Sdx4TyrngdI*

Introduction: No introduction. Starts right away.

Measures:

FIRST STEP
Hora Step

1	Step R to rt (ct 1), step L behind R (ct 2)
2	Step on R (ct 1), lift L (ct 2)
3	Step on L (ct 1), lift R (ct 2)
4	Place toes diag together with heels spread (ct 1)
	Cick heels together (ct 2)
5-8	Repeat meas 1-4
9-16	Repeat meas 1-8

SECOND STEP
Back pas de bas (dance on toes)

1	Jump on R to rt (ct 1), step L behind R (ct &),
	Step on R in place (ct 2)
2	Repeat meas 1 opp dir, opp ft

Sevens to rt

3	Step on R to rt (ct 1), step L behind R (ct &)
	Step on R to rt (ct 2), step L behind R (ct &)
4	Step on R to rt (ct 1), step L behind R (ct &)
	Step on R in place (ct 2)
5-8	Repeat meas 1-4 opp dir, opp ft
9-16	Repeat meas 1-8

THIRD STEP
Twist step

1	Step R over L, twist body to left (ct 1), lift L while twisting body to rt (ct 2)
2	Step L over R, twist body, face ctr (ct 1), lift R, twist body to face ctr

— 15 —

	(ct 2)
3	Step fwd on R (ct 1), place L next to R (ct 2)
4	Spread heels (ct 1), click heels tog (ct 2)
5	Chug fwd (ct 1), chug back (ct 2)
6	Chug diag fwd left (ct 1), chug back (ct 2)
7	Jump back on R (ct 1), step on L in place (ct &), Step on R in place(ct 2)
8	Turn diag left, leap onto L (ct 1), diag stamp R next to L (ct 2)
9-16	Repeat meas 1-8

ORDER OF STEPS

1. First Step: 2x, Second Step: 2x, Third Step: 2x
2. First Step: 4x, Second Step: 2x, Third Step: 2x
3. First Step: 4x, Second Step: 2x, Third Step: 2x

BELO LITSE LYUBAM (MACEDONIA)

Dance Meaning: I like (love) a beautiful face
Pronunciation: Belo Litse Lyoubam
Choreography: By Jim Gold in Macedonian folk dance style
Music: Duquesne University Tamburitzans
Formation: Line, hands in W positions
Meter: 2/4
Jim Gold YouTube video: *http://bit.ly/2De6La3*
Introduction: 8 measures: (Or/and) dance 3rd step
Measures:

FIRST STEP
Moving LOD (CCW) while facing slightly front

1	Step R (ct 1), step L (ct 2)
2	Step R (ct 1), lift L (ct 2)
3	Step on L (ct 1), lift R (ct 2)
4	Face front: Step on R to side (ct 1), close L to R (ct 2)

SECOND STEP
Two 2-steps

1	R (ct 1), L (ct &), R (ct 2)
2	L (ct 1), R (ct &), L (ct 2)

Grapevine: 4

3	R (ct 1), step L behind R (ct 2)
4	Step R to rt (ct 1), cross L over R (ct 2)

Cherkessia: 8

5	Step fwd on R (ct 1), step on L in place (ct 2)
6	Step back on R (ct 1), step on L in place (ct 2)
7-8	Repeat meas 1-2

THIRD STEP
Into ctr

1	R (ct 1), L (ct 2)
2	R (ct 1), lift L (ct 2)

Back out of ctr

3	L (ct 1), R (ct 2)
4	L (ct 1), tch R next to L (ct 2)
5-8	Repeat meas 1-4

ORDER OF STEPS
1. First Step: 2x, Second Step: 3x, Third Step: 1x
2. First Step: 2x, Second Step: 3x, Third Step: 1x
3. First Step: 2x, Second Step: 3x

BOIEREASCA HORA (ROMANIA)

Dance Meaning: Boiereasca refers to boyar who was a member of the highest rank
   of the feudal Bulgarian, Kievan, Moscovian, Serbian, Wallachian,
   Moldavian, and later Romanian aristocracies.
Pronunciation: Boy ar eska
Choreography: By Jim Gold in Romanian folk dance style
Music: Unknown
Formation: Open circle, hands in W position
Meter: 4/4
Jim Gold YouTube video: *https://www.youtube.com/watch?v=-GM57ljKJv4*
Introduction: Starts right away
Measures:

FIRST STEP 3x
Into ctr
1   R (ct 1), L (ct 2), R (ct 3), tch L (ct 4)
2   Back: L (ct 1), R (ct 2), L (ct 3). tch R (ct 4)
3   Moving to rt: R (ct 1), . L behind R (ct 2), step on R (ct 3),
     lift L (ct 4)
4   Moving to lft: L (ct 1), close R next to L (ct 2), step L to lft (ct 3),
     lift R (ct 4)

SECOND STEP
Grapevine
1-2   7's grapevine to rt: start on R, end lift L
3-4   7's grapevine lft, start on L, end lift R

THIRD STEP
Five Cherkesia
1   Step on R (ct 1), cross L over R (ct 2), step R in place (ct 3), step L
     next to R (ct 4)
2   Cross R over L (ct 1), step L in place (ct 2), stamp on R and stay
     (ct 3-4)
     (Optional: cherkesia 9 steps starting with R)
3   Step on L (ct 1), cross R over L (ct 2), step L in place (ct 3), step R
     next to L (ct 4)
4   Cross L over R (ct 1), step R in place (ct 2), stamp on L and stay
     (ct 3-4)
     (Optional: cherkesia 9 steps starting with L)

ORDER OF STEPS
1. First Step: 3x, Second Step: 2x Third Step: 2x

BOIEREASCA JIM (ROMANIA)

Dance Meaning: Jim's Boyar
Pronunciation: Boy ar eska
Choreography: By Jim Gold in Romanian folk dance style
Music: Unknown
Formation: Open circle, hands in W position
Meter: 4/4
YouTube video: *http://bit.ly/2oNRV5i*
Introduction: 4 measures
Measures:

FIRST STEP (PART I)
Moving LOD, Triangle step: Diag fwd and back

1   Diag into ctr: R (ct 1), L (ct 2), R (ct 3), tch L (ct 4)
2   Diag out of ctr: L (ct 1), R (ct 2). L (ct 3), tch R (ct 4)
3   **Grapevine and touches: LOD CCW**
     Step R to rt (ct 1), step L behind R (ct 2)
     step R to rt (ct3), step L front of R (ct 4)
4   Step R to rt (ct 1), tap L next to R (ct 2)
     Step L to lft (ct 3). Tap R next to L (ct 4)

ORDER OF STEPS:
1. First Step only

BUSK (NORWAY)

Dance Meaning: Bush, shrub
Pronunciation: Boosk
Choreography: By Jim Gold using traditional steps from Norway
Music: Majorstuen
Formation: Line, arms in V position.
Meter: 4/4
Jim Gold YouTube video: *https://www.youtube.com/watch?v=Bh2aWgG7cC8*
Introduction: 8 measures
Measures:

FIRST STEP
Walk 4 steps to the right, CCW
1   R (ct 1), L(ct 2), R(ct 3), L(ct 4)
     Continue in LOD with a schottishe step
2   Step R (ct 1), step L (ct &), step R (ct 2)
     Hop on R (ct &), step L (ct 3), step R (ct &), step L (ct 4), hop on L (ct &)
3   Face ctr: Step R to right side (ct 1)
     Step L next to R (ct &)
     Step on R (ct 2), hop on R (ct &)
     Place L ft next to R calf (ct &)
     Step L to left side (ct 3), step R next to L (ct &)
     Step on L (ct 4), hop on L (ct &)
     Grapevine to left: CW
4   Step R over L (ct 1), step L next to R (ct &)
     Step R behind L (ct 2), step L to left (ct 3)
     Place R next to L (ct 4)
5-8   Repeat meas 1-4

SECOND STEP
Face ctr
1   Step R to right side (ct 1), step L next to R (ct &), step on R (ct 2)
     Hop on R, place L ft next to R calf (ct &)
     Step L to left side (ct 3), step R next to L (ct &), step on L (ct 4)
     Hop on L, push R ft diag to R side, point R toe (ct &)
     Hornpipe rocking step
2   Cross R over L, place weight on R, rock fwd on R (ct 1), rock back on L (ct 2)

Rock fwd on R (ct 3), rock back on L (ct &)
Rock fwd on R (ct 4), rock back on L (ct &)

3   **Into ctr**
Step fwd on R (ct 1), fwd on L (ct 2)
Place-stamp R ft in third ballet position (instep of foot by ankle next to left foot (ct 3)
half turn to right on R heel and L toe, face out of circle (ct 4)

4   Moving out of ctr repeat meas 3
Repeat Second Step twice

ORDER OF STEPS
1.   First Step: 1x , Second Step: 2x
Continue pattern until end

CAN KIZ (TURKEY)

Dance Meaning: Soul (or spirit) of a Girl
Pronunciation: Jon kuz
Choreography: By Jim Gold in Turkish folk dance style
Music: Dunav Tours: Antalia 2005 with Ersin Seyhan
Formation: Tight line
Meter: 2/4
Jim Gold YouTube video: *https://www.youtube.com/watch?v=CpKH2vTs7K4*
Introduction: 8 measures
Measures:

FIRST STEP
Moving to the right, holding hands, arms tight at sides, shake shoulders:

1   Step to R (ct 1), close L to R (ct 2)
2   Repeat meas 1
3   Repeat meas 1
4   Repeat meas 1
5-8   Repeat meas 1-4

SECOND STEP
Moving to the left, holding hands, arms tight at sides

1   Step to R (ct 1), stamp L next to R (ct 2)
2   Step L to left (ct 1), close R to L (ct 2)
3   Repeat meas 2
4   Step L to left (ct 1), close R to L (ct &) step L to left
5-12   Repeat meas 1-4 2x

THIRD STEP
Into ctr, shaking shoulders

1   Step R fwd (ct 1), step L fwd (ct 2)
2   Step R fwd (ct 1), tch L onto floor next to R(ct 2)
Back out from ctr: shaking shoulders
3   Step back on L (ct 1), step back on R (ct 2)
4   Step back on L (ct 1), tch R onto floor next to L (ct 2)
5-8   Repeat meas 1-4

FOURTH STEP

      Walk 4 steps to the right

1-2   R (ct 1), L(ct 2), R (ct1), L (ct 2)

3-4   **Walk in a full CCW circle 4 steps (right turn)**

      R (ct 1), L(ct 2), R (ct 1), L (ct 2)

      Walk into ctr 3 steps and lift L

5-6   R(ct 1), L(ct 2), R(ct 1), lift L (ct 2)

      First ending

7-8   Walk back 3 steps, stamp R next to L

      L (ct 1), R (ct 2), L (ct 1) stamp R next to L (ct 2)

9-14   Repeat meas 1-6

15-16 **Second ending**

      Walk back 2 steps: R (ct 1), L (ct 2)

      "Shimmy bounce-bounce" step

      Place both feet together and shimmy (ct 1)

      Bounce twice on both ft: (ct 2, ct &)

ORDER OF STEPS

First step: 1x, Second step: 3x, Third Step: 2x, Fourth Step: 2x

First step: 1x, Second step: 3x, Third Step: 2x, Fourth Step: 3x

First step: 1x, Second step: 3x, Third Step: 2x, Fourth Step: 1x

CANTIGA DEUS MADRE (Spain)

Dance Meaning: Songs of Saint Mary, Cantiga 322, Mother God
Name: A Virgen, que de Deus Madre: in Gallico-Portuguese language from
 medieval Spain.
Source: Created from 13th century music: Cantigas de Santa Maria, Cantiga 322.
 Folk dance steps from northern Spain.
Music: Sendebar: Medieval Music of the Mediterranean
Choreography: By Jim Gold using traditional steps from medieval Spain
Formation: Open circle
Mood/Style: Haunting, ghostly, spirits hovering
Meter: 4/4
Jim Gold YouTube video: *https://www.youtube.com/watch?v=8g2VLJmEeEA*
Introduction: slow intro. Then 16 measures of music
Measures:

FIRST STEP
Face rt (LOD)

1   Step R (ct 1), step L (ct 2)
      Face ctr: Step R (ct3), bring L behind R (ct &)
      Step R in place (ct 4), stamp L next to R (ct &)

2   Step L (ct 1), tch R toe straight fwd (ct &)
      Step R (ct2), tch L toe straight fwd (ct &)
      Step L to lft (ct 3), step R behind L (ct &)
      Step on L (ct 4), tap R heel next to L (ct &)

3-12   Repeat meas 1-2 4x (or leader decides)

SECOND STEP
Into ctr

1   Step R fwd (ct 1), step L fwd (ct 2)
      R fwd (ct 3), L next to R (ct &), R (ct 4), stamp L (ct &)

2   Step L (ct 1), tch R fwd (ct &), step R (ct 2), tch L fwd (ct &)
      Step back on L (ct 3), step back on R (ct &)
      Step on L (ct 4), tap R next to L (ct &)

3-8   Repeat meas 1-2 4x (Or leader decides)

Third Step (Optional)
Into ctr

1   Step R fwd (ct 1), step L fwd (ct 2)
      R fwd (ct3), L next to R (ct &), R (ct 4)

Sevens: Facing ctr. Moving back out of ctr: "back rida"

2   Step back and up on L (ct 1), step R next to L as you step down (ct &), Counts 2-4: Repeat count 1 3x

3-4   Repeat meas 1-2 2x (or leader decides)

ORDER OF STEPS

1. First Step: 4x, Second Step: 4x

    Or leader calls changes

CANTIGAS DE SANTA MARIA: CANTIGA I (SPAIN)

Dance Meaning: Songs of Saint Mary. Song 1
Name: Des oge mais quer eu trobar: Gallico-Portuguese language from medieval Spain.
Source: Created by Jim Gold based on 13ᵗʰ century folk dance steps from northern Spain.
Music: Sendebar: Medieval Music of the Mediterranean
Choreography: By Jim Gold using traditional steps from medieval Spain
Formation: Circle
Meter: 4/4
Jim Gold YouTube video: *https://www.youtube.com/watch?v=C6B77So0At8*
Introduction: 2 measures
Measures:

FIRST STEP
Rida: Moving to left, CW. Arms in V position

1   Cross R over L (ct 1), bring L next to R (ct 2)
     cross R over L (3), bring L next to R (ct 4)

2   Grapevine step: step R in front of L (ct 1)
     Step L next to R (ct 2)
     Step R behind L (ct 3)
     L to right (ct 4).

3-4   Repeat meas 1-2

5-6   Repeat meas 1-2

7-8   Repeat meas 1-2

SECOND STEP

1   Step forward on R (ct 1-2)
     Step L next to R (ct 3-4)

2   Step back on L (ct 1-2)
     Step R next to L (ct 3-4)
     4 front pas de bas

3   Step on R in place (ct 1), cross L over R (ct &)
     Step on R in place (ct 2)
     Step on L in place (ct 3), cross R over L (ct &)
     Step on L in place (ct 4)

4   Repeat meas 3
     Walk 3 steps right, CCW

5   Step R (ct 1-2)

Step L (ct 3-4)

6   Step R (ct 1-2), touch L heel across R leg (ct 3-4)

7   Walk 3 steps left, CW: step L (ct 1-2), step R (ct 3-4)

8   Step L (ct 1-2), step on R next to L facing ctr (ct 3-4)

9   Step into ctr on R (ct 1-2), touch L toe on floor behind R (ct 3-4)

10   Step back on L (ct 1-2), step on R in place (ct 3-4)

4-step full turn left, CCW, arms in W position, snap fingers to imitate sound of castanets

11   R (ct 1-2), L (ct 3-4)

12   R (ct 1-2), L (ct 3-4)

CĂSUTA NOASTRĂ (ROMANIA)

Dance Meaning: Our house
Pronunciation: Dgikuh Petrescoo
Choreography: By Jim Gold in Romanian folk dance style
Music: Sung by Gic Petrescu: *http://bit.ly/2CWAOTM*
Thank you Manuela Schuster and Paula Mondschein
Formation: Open circle
Meter: 4/4
Jim Gold YouTube video: *https://www.youtube.com/watch?v=3pSDDS2XMjI*
Introduction: 4 measures, then dance meas 5-8 of First Step
Measures

FIRST STEP
Into ctr and back

1   Step fwd on R (ct 1), fwd on L (ct 2), fwd on R (ct 3), tch L toe next to R (ct 4)

2   Step back on L (ct 1), back on R (ct 2), back on L (ct 3), tch R toe next to L (ct 4)

3   Step R to rt (ct 1), tch flat L ft lightly next to R (ct 2), step on L (ct 3), lift R (ct 4)
4 step grapevine CW

4   Cross R over L (ct 1), step L to lft (ct 2), step R behind L (ct 3), close L to R (ct 4)

5-8   Repeat meas 1-4

SECOND STEP
Facing CCW: Two 2 steps CCW

1   R (ct 1), L (ct &), R (ct 2). L (ct 3), R (ct &), L (ct 4)
Grapevine 4 CCW

2   Step R to rt (ct 1), step L behind R (ct 2),
Step R to rt (ct 3), step L in front of R (ct 4)

3   Step on R (ct 1), lift L (ct 2), step on L (ct 3)
Push R out pointing and looking at toe (ct 4)
Moving CW

4   Cross R front of L (ct 1), step L behind R but slightly fwd (ct 2)
Cross R front of L (ct 3), close L to R (ct 4)

5-7   Repeat meas 1-3
4-step turn CW

8   R (ct 1), L (ct 2), R (ct 3), L (ct 4)

ORDER OF STEPS

1. First Step: 1x, Second Step: 1x
2. First Step: 1x, Second Step: with gypsy turn1x
3. First Step: 1x, Second Step: 1x
      a. First Step 4 meas
4. First Step: 1x, Second Step: 1x
5. First Step: 1x Second Step: with gypsy turn ending: 1x

Words to Song in Romanian and English

Casuta Noastra

Ca sa mi te fac nevasta
Am dus viata de napasta
Si cu lumea m-am certat
Ca o garofita in glastra
Inflorea casuta noastra
Dar tu draga ai plecat

Casuta noastra
Cuibusor de nebunii
Te asteapta ca sa vii
Casuta noastra
Unde-ntai ne-am sarutat
Plange doru' ne-ncetat

Pentru o salba de margele
Apucasi pe drumuri rele
Nimeni nu te-a suparat
Mi-ai lasat ca bucurie
Doru' care ma sfasie
Si un suflet intristat

Casuta noastra
Cuibusor de nebunii
Te asteapta ca sa vii
Casuta noastra
Unde-ntai ne-am sarutat
Plange doru' neincetat

De-ai sa vii draga fetita
Am sa-ti iau fusta pestrita
Ca sa crape lumea zau
O naframa matasoasa
Tu sa fii cea mai frumoasa
Si mai mandra-n satul tau

Casuta noastra
Cuibusor de nebunii
Te asteapta ca sa vii
Casuta noastra
Unde-ntai ne-am sarutat
Plange doru' neïncetat

Our Cottage

To make you my wife,
I lived a disastrous life,
And I quarreled with the world,
Like a picotee in a vase,
Our cottage flourished,
But you my dear left

Our cottage,
Love nest,
Is waiting for you to come,
Our cottage,
Where we first kissed,
Longing is crying ceaseless

For a necklace of beads,
I went on bad roads,
Nobody upset you,
You've left me as joy
Longing that rips me
And a grieved soul

Our cottage,
Love nest,
Is waiting for you to come,
Our cottage,

Where we first kissed,
Longing is crying ceaseless
For you to come dear girl
I'll buy you a mottled skirt
So the world bursts with envy
And silk handkerchief
You'll be the most beautiful
And most proud in your village

Our cottage,
Love nest,
Is waiting for you to come,
Our cottage,
Where we first kissed,
Longing is crying ceaseless.

CIJA KOLA (CROATIA—SLAVONIA)

Dance Meaning: Whose car (or cart)
Pronunciation: ci ya kola
Choreography: By Jim Gold in Croatian (Slavonian) folk style
Music:
Formation: Open circle moving counter clockwise
Meter: 3/4
Jim Gold YouTibe video: *https://www.youtube.com/watch?v=8Nut9-2a4VM*
Introduction: Start with meas 5 (Or start right away.)
Measures:

FIRST STEP
Waltz step
1   Into ctr R (ct 1), L next to R (ct 2), R in place (ct 3)
2   Back on L (ct 1), R next to L (ct 2), L in place (ct 3)
3-8   Repeat meas 1-2, 3x

SECOND STEP
Rida
1   Down of R (ct 1), L (ct 2) R (ct 3)
2   Up on L (ct 1). RL etc
3-8   Repeat meas 1-2, 3x

Optional: Lift step
5   Lift R (ct 1), step on R in LOD (ct 2), step L next to R (ct 3)
6-8   Repeat meas 5 3x
9-12 **Rida**: Repeat meas 1-4

Optional: Running
13   Run 6 small steps R,L,R,L,R,L
13-16 Repeat meas 1 3x

ORDER OF STEPS
First step: 1x
Second Step: 2x

CIKO IANIKO (BOSNIA)

Dance Meaning: Little Ian
Pronunciation: Tchiko Yaniko
Choreography: By Jim Gold in Bosnian folk style
Music: Flory Jagoda: La Nona Kanata
Formation: Open circle, arms in W position
Meter: 2/4
Jim Gold YouTube video: *https://www.youtube.com/watch?v=Sds3QGgYrgc*
Introduction: 4 measures
Measures:

FIRST STEP
Into ctr and back
1	Step fwd on R (ct 1), L (ct 2)
2	R (ct 1), lift L (ct 2)
3	Step back on L (ct 1), R (ct 2)
4	3 steps in place L (ct 1), R (ct &), L (ct 2)
5-7	Repeat meas 1-3
8	4 steps in place L (ct 1), R (ct &), L (ct 2), R (ct &)

SECOND STEP
Ccw grapevine and two-2-steps
1	Step L front of R (ct 1), step R next to L (ct 2)
2	Step L behind R (ct 1), step R next to L (ct 2)
3-4	Repeat meas, 1-2

Two 2-steps
5	Facing CCW, step fwd R to rt (ct 1), L next to R (ct &) Step R in place (ct 2)
6	Repeat meas 5 opp ft
7	Repeat meas 1
8	Step L behind R (ct 1), tch L softly next to R (ct 2)

THIRD STEP
CCW grapevine 7, step. light stamp
1	Step R to rt (ct 1), L behind (ct 2)
2	R to rt (ct 1), L in fron t(ct 2)
3	Ste R to rt (ct 1), L behind (ct 2)
4	Step R to rt (ct 1) soft stamp L next to R (ct 2)

ORDER OF STEPS
1. First Step: 1x, Second Step: 1x, Third Step: 1x

DANCE OF THE FIREMEN (Romania)

Choreography: By Jim Gold in Romanian folk dance style
Style: Drunken style
Music: Tarif de Haidouks, Dance of the Firemen
Formation: Open circle, shoulder hold
Meter: 4/4
Jim Gold YouTube video: *https://www.youtube.com/watch?v=gDa9QUZisdw*
Introduction: 12 measures
Measures:

FIRST STEP

Moving to right, CCW

1	Step on R (ct 1), step on L behind R (ct 2)
2	Repeat measure 1
3	Step on R to R side (ct 1), stamp-brush L in place
	Lean fwd in drunken stumble (ct 2)
4	Step hard, (fall) drunken style forward on L (ct 1-2)

Moving to left, CW

5	Cross R over L (ct 1), step on L (ct 2)
6	Repeat measure 5
7	Step on R across L (ct 1), step on L (ct 2)
8	Touch R heel next to L (ct 1-2)
9	During extra measure, first two times through
	Step-lean in drunken style slightly forward on R (ct 1-2)

DE BOCA DEL DYO (BOSNIA)

Dance Meaning: From The Mouth of God
Choreography: By Jim Gold in Judeo/Bosnian folk dance style
Music: Flory Jagoda. Sung in Ladino language
Formation: Open circle, low hands, V position
Meter: 2/4
Jim Gold YouTube video: https://www.youtube.com/watch?v=K7Zan0bGn_Q
Introduction: 2 meas
Measures:

FIRST STEP
Hands down (V pos)

1	Step R to rt (ct 1), stamp L next to R (ct &)
	Step L to lft (ct 2), stamp R next to L (ct &)
2	Step R to R (ct 1), step L behind R (ct &)
	Step R to rt (2), stamp L next to R (ct &)
3-4	Repeat meas 1 opp ft opp dir
5-8	Repeat meas 1-4

SECOND STEP
Rocking 4's, hands down (V pos)

1	Step R fwd, lean fwd (ct 1), stamp L next to R (ct &)
	Step L back, lean back (ct 2), stamp R next to L (ct &)
2	Step R fwd, lean fwd (ct 1), stamp L next to R (ct &)
	Step L back, lean back (ct 2), stamp R next to L (ct &)

1/2 turn 7's (CW), arms out, parallel to floor/shldr height, palms up

3	Step on R (ct 1), step on L (ct &)
	Step on R (ct 2), step on L (ct &)
4	Step on R (ct 1), step on L (ct &)
	Step on R (ct 2)

Facing out of circle: Rocking 4/s, arms out

5	Step L back, lean back (ct 1), stamp R next to L (ct &)
	Step R fwd, lean fwd (ct 2), stamp L next to R (ct &)
6	Repeat meas 5
7-8	**1/2 turn 7's (CCW), arms out**
	Repeat meas 3-4, opp ft, opp dir.

THIRD STEP
7 steps into ctr, hands reaching up, open and close

Hands raised, finger push up: "naches from God" step.

1 Step ctr on R, both hands raised, fingers push up (ct 1)
Step L behind R, close fingers (ct &)
Step into ctr, both hands raised, fingers push up (ct 2)
Step L behind R, close fingers to palms (ct &)

2 Step into ctr, both hands raised, fingers push up (ct 1)
Step L behind R, close fingers to palms (ct &)
Step into ctr, both hands raised, fingers push up (ct 2)
Clap hands (ct &)

3 **7 steps of out of ctr, off-beat claps**
Step back on L (ct 1), step R next to L and clap (ct &)
Step back on L (ct 2), step R next to L and clap (ct &)

4 Step back on L (ct 1), step R next to L and clap (ct &)
Step back on L (ct 2), step R next to L and clap (ct &)

Fourth Step (Transition or ending step)

1 Step R to rt (ct 1), close L to R (ct 2)
Step L to lft (ct 3), close R to L (ct 4)

ORDER OF STEPS

1. First Step: 2x, Second Step: 1x, Third Step: 1x, Fourth Step: 1x
2. First Step: 2x, Second Step: 1x, Third Step: 1x, Fourth Step: 1x
3. First Step: 2x, Second Step: 1x, Third Step: 1x, Fourth Step: 1x

DJENI ME MAMO (BALANCE DANCE—BULGARIA)

Dance Meaning: Marry me, Mother
Pronunciation: DJEN-i Me Mamo
Choreography: By Jim Gold in West Bulgarian folk dance style
Source: Pirin Region, Lesnoto style
Music: Peroun: Posloushaite Patrioti. Djeni Me Mamo
Formation: Open circle, arms in W position.
Meter: First step: 7/8: and 2/4 slow/quick/quick: s, q, q
Jim Gold YouTube video: *https://www.youtube.com/watch?v=Wza0lMLJn0U*
Introduction: 4 measures.
Measures:

FIRST STEP: 2/4

2 two-step to the right, CCW

1	R(q), L(q), R (s)
2	L(q), R(q), L (s)

4 crossing steps to the left, CW

3   Cross R over L (ct 1), step L next to R (ct &)
        Cross R over L (ct 2)), step L next to R (ct &)

3-step grapevine

4   R in front (ct 1), L to left side of R (ct &)
        Step R behind L (ct 2)
        Step on L while turning to face CW (ct &)

5-7   Repeat meas 1-3
8   Step R behind L (ct 2)
        Step on L next to R (ct &)

SECOND STEP: 7/8

1   Step R to right side (s), lift L across R (q), step on L across R (q),
2   Step R to right(s), lift L and hold steady, motionless (q, q),
3   Stay in holding position balancing on R leg,

Two dips on R

        Dip on R leg, dip (q, q),
4   Bring leg left behind R knee (s, q), step on L ft (q),
5   Lift R, hook R around behind Left knee (q, q).
6-15   Repeat meas 1-5 2x

ORDER OF STEPS
1. First Step: 1x, Second Step: 1x
2. First Step: 1x, Second Step: 1x
3. First Step: 1x, Second step: 1x
4. First Step: 1x, Second Step: 1x

DOLA MOJ DOLA (ALBANIA)

Dance Meaning: I'm coming out (said to a woman) Moj—used to call a woman (calling a man use "mor").

Pronunciation: Dola moee dola

Choreography: Jim Gold in Albanian folk dance style

Music: Albanian CD: Maya: Dola moj dola

Formation: Open circle, arms down in V position

Meter: 2/4

Jim Gold YouTube video: *https://www.youtube.com/watch?v=B7mzrSI1Nyk*

Introduction: 4 meas, then dance Third Step 1x.

Measures:

FIRST STEP
4 pogonishte CCW

1	R (ct 1-2). L (ct 3), R (ct 4)
2	L (ct 1-2), R (ct 3), L (ct 4)
3-4	Repeat meas 1-2

2 back pas de bas

5	Step R to rt(ct 1-2), step L behind R (ct 3), step R in place (ct 4)
6	Repeat meas 5 opp ft opp dir
7	Fwd on R (ct 1-2), step L next to R (ct 3-4)
8	Back L (ct 1-2), tch R toe to L ft (ct 3-4)
9-16	Repeat meas 1-8

SECOND STEP
Into Ctr

1	Step fwd on R (ct 1), step L next to R (ct 2)
	Step fwd on R (ct 3,4) pushing open hands slightly rt
2	Step fwd on L (ct 1), step R next to L (ct 2)
	Step fwd on L (ct 3,4) pushing open hands slightly lft

Out of ctr

3	Step back R (ct 1-2), step back on L (ct 3-4) push open hand down
4	Back on R, slap R thigh (ct 1),back L, slap L thigh (ct 2)
	Back on R, slap R thigh (ct 3),back L, slap L thigh (ct 4)
5-8	Repeat meas 1-4, 3x
9-16	Repeat meas 1-8

THIRD STEP: Transition (PART III)
Fwd and back

| 1 | Fwd on R (ct 1), step L next to R (ct 2), step on R (ct 3-4) |
| 2 | Back L (ct 1), step R next to L (ct 2), step L next to R (ct 3-4) |

2 back pas de bas

3	Step R to rt (ct 1-2), L next to R (ct 3-4)
4	Step L to lft (ct 1-2), R next to L (ct 3-4)
5-7	Repeat meas 1-3
8	Step L to lft (ct 1-2), tch R toe next to L (ct 3-4)

ORDER OF STEPS

1. First Step: 1x, Second Step: 1x, Third Step: 1x
2. First Step: 1x, Second Step: 1x, Third Step: 1x
3. First Step: 1x. Second Step:
4. Ending: Third Step: meas 1 and meas 8

   (Fwd on R(ct 1-2), step L next to R(ct 3-4)

   Back L(ct 1-2). tch R toe next to L(ct 3-4))

DONKE LESNOTO (BULGARIA)

Dance Meaning: Donke's Dance
Pronunciation: Donka Les-NO-to
Choreography: By Jim Gold in Macedonian-Bulgarian folk dance style
Source: Pirin region of Bulgaria; Lesnoto style
Music: Bulgaria
Formation: Open circle
Meter: 7/8: slow/quick/quick: s, q, q
Jim Gold YouTube video: *https://www.youtube.com/watch?v=u4V503xRnpU*
Introduction: 10 measures
Measures:

FIRST STEP
Basic lesnoto
1   Step on R (s), lift L (q), step on L over R (q)
2   Repeat meas 1
3   Step on R (s), lift L (q, q)
4   Step on L (s), lift R (q, q)
5   Twist R to left (s), twist R back to ctr (q, q).
6-20   Repeat meas 1-5 3x

SECOND STEP
Forward lifts
1   Step into ctr on R (s, q, q)
2   Step back on L, lift R high (s, q, q)
3   Hook R ft. behind L knee in big sweeping motion (s, q, q)
4   Step on R (s), bounce on both ft (q, q)
5   Hold legs together, twist knees to L in a small circle (s, q, q)
6-10   Repeat meas 1-5

THIRD STEP
Face ctr but moving to the right, CCW
1   Step on R(s), lift L (q), cross L over R, step on L (q)
2   Repeat meas 1
3   Repeat meas 1
4   Step on R (s), touch L heel to left side (q)
     Touch L heel diag left ctr (q)
5   Step on L ft (s), touch R heel diagonal ctr right side (q)
     Touch R heel diagonal ctr again (q)
6-10   Repeat meas 1-5

DREIDEL COCEK (EASTERN EUROPE/KLEZMER NOVELTY DANCE)

Dance Meaning: Spinning Top Cocek
Pronunciation: Draydel Tchotchek
Choreography: By Jim Gold in Macedonian and Klezmer folk dance style
Music: Erran Baron Cohen presents Songs in the Key of Hanukkah
Formation: Open circle
Meter: 2/4
Jim Gold YouTube video: *https://www.youtube.com/watch?v=gDeBFjvdX8w*
Introduction: 8 measures
Measures:

FIRST STEP

Dreidel Cocek: Moving to the right, diag back and fwd
(A three-measure dance step against a four-measure count)

1	Step diag back on R (ct 1), step diag back on L (ct 2)
2	Step diag back on R (ct 1), step on L in place, change directions to face diag right (ct 2), step on R in place (ct &)
3	Step diag fwd on L (ct 1), step on R in place (ct 2) Step on L in place (ct &)
4-15	Repeat meas 1-3 5x
16	End with step R to right (ct 1), bring L next to R (ct 2)

SECOND STEP

Klezmer Style:

1	Cross R in front of L (ct 1), step on L in place (ct 2)
2	Step on R next to L (ct 1), step on L in place (ct 2)
3-4	Repeat meas 1

Push arms

5	Moving to right: Step on R, push arms fwd (ct 1) Step on L behind, bring arms back (ct 2)
6	Step on R to right, push arms fwd (ct 1) Step on L, bring arms back (ct 2)

Big lift L

7	Step on R (ct 1), big lift L (ct 2)
8	Cross L over R, step on L(ct 1), step on R (no weight) next to L (ct 2)
9-16	Repeat meas 1-8

DVASHTIM, TRITSIM (BULGARIA)

Dance Meaning: Two times, Three times
Pronunciation: DVASH-tim, TRI-tsim
Choreography: By Jim Gold in Bulgarian folk dance style
Source: Plovdiv Region
Music: Vievska Folk Group
Formation: Open circle
Meter: 9/8: quick/quick/quick/slow: q, q, q, s
Jim Gold YouTube video: *http://bit.ly/2B9IAHT*
Introduction: 8 measures
Measures:

FIRST STEP

1	Into ctr. R (q), L (q), R (q), touch L fwd (s)
2	Back out: L (q), R (q),L (q), touch R toe next to L (s)

Grapevine to the right, CCW

3	Step to R (q), L behind (q), R to R side (q), L in front (s)
4	R to R side (q), L behind (q), R to R side (q). Step on L next to R (s)
5-8	Repeat meas 1-4

SECOND STEP

Moving CW

1	Step L to lft (q), step R behind L (q), step on L and lift R (q), stamp R (s)

8-step grapevine to the right, CCW

2	Step R to rt (q), L behind R (q), R to rt (q), L in front R (s)
3	Step R to rt (q). Step L behind R (q), step R to rt (q), close L to R (s)3
4	Repeat meas 1
5-6	Repeat meas 2-3
7	Repeat meas 1
8	Step R to rt (q), step L next to R (q), step R to rt (q), close L to R (s)

ORDER OF STEPS

1. First Step: 2x, Second Step: 2x
2. First Step: 2x, Second Step: 2x
3. First Step: 2x, Second Step: 2x
4. First Step: 2x, Ending: meas 1-2 of STEP TWO

EASY WINNERS (USA)

Choreography: By Jim Gold in Ragtime/American folk dance style
Music: Scott Joplin
Style: Jaunty, free, arms loose
Formation: Open Circle, hands free
Meter: 2/4
Jim Gold YouTube video: *https://www.youtube.com/watch?v=pq2Q9qJKjoQ*
Introduction: 4 measures
Measures:

FIRST STEP

Strutting Walk: 15 walking steps, thumbs through suspenders, strutting style

1	R (ct 1), L (ct 2)
2-7	Repeat meas 1 6x
8	R (ct 1), bring L next to R (ct &),
	Heel stand step: With ft together go back on heels, stand on both heels (ct 2).
9-16	Repeat First Step

SECOND STEP

6 two-steps CCW, arms moving free style

1	Step diag forward CCW on R (ct 1) , bring L behind R (ct &)
	Step on R diag forward again (ct 2) , brush/kick L diag forward (ct &)
2	Repeat meas CCW with opp ft
3-6	Repeat meas 1 and 2 2x

Four Elephant Flop-Walk steps, thumbs through suspenders, strutting style

7	Step R heel forward with straight R leg (ct 1)
	Bend R knee, flatten R ft, as you bring L ft up behind R heel (ct &)
	Step R heel forward with straight R leg (ct 2)
	Bend R knee, flatten R ft, as you bring L ft up behind R heel (ct &)
8	Step R heel forward with straight R leg (ct 1)
	Bend R knee, flatten R ft, as you bring L ft up behind R heel (ct &)
	Step R heel forward with straight R leg (ct 2)
	Bend R knee, flatten R ft, as you bring L ft up behind R heel (ct &)
9-16	Repeat Second Step

THIRD STEP (Plain)

1-2	Into ctr: R (ct 1), L (ct 2), R (ct 1), kick L (ct 2)
3-4	Back out: L (ct 1), R (ct 2), L (ct 1) , step R next to L ct 2)

Suzie Q step

5-6	Toes out (ct 1-2), toes in (ct 1-2)
7-8	Toes out(ct 1), toes in(ct 2), toes out (ct 1), toes in (ct 2)

3-step walk into ctr and tch

9-10	R (ct 1), L (ct 2), R (ct 1), tch L fwd (ct 2)

3-step walk back

11-12	Back out: L (ct 1), R (ct 2), L (ct 1), close R next to L(ct 2)

Suzie Q, double time Suzie Q

13-14	Toes out (ct 1-2), toes in (ct 1-2)

Double time Suzie Q

15	Toes out (ct 1), toes in (ct &), toes out (ct 2), toes in (ct &)
16	Repeat meas 7

FOURTH STEP (Fancy)

1-4	Repeat meas 1-4 of Third Step
5-6	Suzie Q: toes out (ct 1-2), toes in (ct 1-2)
7-8	Toes out (ct 1), clap toes of both feet together (ct 2), clap again (ct &).
9-10	Into ctr: R (ct 1), L (ct 2), R(ct 1), touch L (ct 2)
11-12	Back out: L (ct 1), R (ct 2), L (ct 1), step R next to L(ct 2)
13-14	Suzie Q: toes out (ct 1-2), toes in (ct 1-2)

One-Legged Double Time Suzie Q

15	Move to right, CCW: R toe out (ct 1) R toe in (ct &), R toe out(ct 2), R toe in(&)
16	R toe out (ct 1), snap-slide L ft next to R ft (ct 2).

ORDER OF STEPS

First Step: 2x, Second Step: 2x, Third Step: 1x, Fourth Step: 1x,
First Step: 2x
Break: Bell ringing 4 meas
Second Step: 2x, Third Step: 1x, Fourth Step: 1x,
First Step: 2x, Second Step: 2x, Fourth Step: 1x

EDELWEISS (AUSTRIA)

Dance Meaning: A white flower found in the Alps, (Leontopodium alpinum) "Edelweiss"

Pronunciation: Edelveis

Choreography: By Jim Gold

Music: From 1959 Rodgers and Hammerstein musical *The Sound of Music* Performed by harmonica virtuoso Avram Barzilay

Formation: Open circle, arms down in V position

YouTube Video: *http://bit.ly/2oGzoop*

Meter: 3/4

Introduction: 4 measures

Measures:

FIRST STEP

Walk 6 steps LOD: Arms down in V position

1	Step R (ct 1), step L (ct 2), step R (ct 3)
2	Step L (ct 1), step R (ct 2), step L (ct 3)
3	Turn CW: R (ct 1), L (ct 2), R (ct 3)
4	**Crossing Step**

Cross L front of rt (ct 1), step on R in place (ct 2)

step L next to R (ct 3)

4 back pas de bas

5	Step on R heel with straight leg (ct 1), rolls to flat ft while stepping on L leg

Step L toe with bent leg (ct 2), slight dip

Step R in place with whole flat ft (ct 3)

6	Repeat meas 5 opp. ft
7	Step fwd on R, bringing arms parallel to floor (ct 1)

Step L next to R (ct 2), step R in place (ct 3)

8	Step back on L, bringing arms down to sides (ct 1)

Step L next to R (ct 2), step R in place (ct 3)

9-16	Repeat meas 1-8

SECOND STEP

Grapevine 7 RLOD

1	Step R over L (ct 1), step L side of rt (ct 2)

Step R behind L (ct 3)

2	Step L to side of rt (ct 1), step R front of L (ct 2)

Step L to side of R (ct 3)

3	Step R behind L (ct 1)
	5-step cherkessia: Step L to side of rt (ct 2), cross R over L(ct 3)
4	Step on L in place (ct 1), step R next to L (ct 2)
	Cross L over R (ct 3)
5-8	Repeat meas 5-8 of FIRST STEP
9-16	Repeat meas 1-8 of SECOND STEP

ORDER OF STEPS
1. First Step: 1x, Second Step: 1x
2. First Step: 1x, Second Step: 1x

EGOSCUE HORA (ROMANIA)

Dance Meaning: (Pete) Egoscue's Hora
Pronunciation: E GOS kyew's Hora
Choreography: By Jim Gold in "Romanian" style playful character dancing
Music: Unknown
Formation: Open circle, hands in V position
Style: Mechanical, stiff, fixed. "Dance of the Mechanical Dolls"
YouTube video link: *http://bit.ly/2oZ2mkR*
Meter: 4/4
Introduction: Starts right away
Measures:

FIRST STEP

16 Sides. "Mechanical doll step" Face: Fixed smile

1   Step R to rt, lean rt (ct 1), close L to R, lean lft (ct 2)
      Step R to rt, lean rt (ct 3), close L to R, lean lft (ct 4)

2-4   Repeat meas 1 3x

5-8   Repeat meas 1-4

SECOND STEP

Cherkesia 16

Face: Normal face

1   Step R front of L (ct 1), step L in place (ct 2)
      Step R back of L (ct 3), step L in place (ct 4)

2-4   Repeat meas 1 3x

THIRD STEP

4 Grapevine CW

Face: Normal face

1   Step R front of L (ct 1), step L to lft (ct 2)
      Step R behind L (ct 3), step L to lft (ct 3)

2-4   Repeat meas 1 3x

FOURTH STEP

Egoscue step: "Race Starting" step: Speeds: moderate, fast, slow, arms free. Step fwd on R ft, with L ft back ("Start race" position.) Arm swinging step: bring hands to side of face (beneath ears). Face: Fixed wide open eyes.

1   R arm fwd, L arm back (ct 1), L arm fwd, R arm back (ct 2)

R arm fwd, L arm back (ct 3), L arm fwd, r arm back (ct 4)

2-4   Repeat meas 1 3x. 1 movement per beat
5-6   Repeat Racing step slow. 1 movements per 2 beats
7-8   Racing step moderate,   2 movements per beat
       Racing step fast
9-11   Repeat meas 1-3
12   Double time, Fast

Further explanations:
   Slow and fast (or low to ground and repeat meas 1-4)
   5   Bring R arm fwd, palm flat, next to face, L arm back hold (ct 1-2),
         Bring R arm back, L arm fwd, palm flat, next to face, hold (ct 3-4)
   6-7   Repeat meas 1 2x
   8   R arm fwd (ct 1), L arm fwd (ct &), R arm fwd (ct 2), L
         arm fwd (ct &), R arm fwd (ct 3), L arm fwd (ct &), R arm fwd
         (ct 4), L arm fwd (ct &)
   9-12 Repeat meas 1-4 (with improvisation, if desired)

ORDER OF STEPS
1. First Step: 1x, Second Step: 1x, Third Step: 1x, Fourth Step: 1x
2. First Step: 1x, Second Step: 1x, Third Step: 1x, Fourth Step A: 1x (meas 1-8)
3. First Step: 1x, Second Step: 1x, Third Step: 1x, Fourth Step: 1x
4. First Step: 1x, Second Step: 1x

EL PASTOR (ARGENTINA)

Dance Meaning: The Shepherd
Choreography: Jim Gold in international folk dance style
Music: Canto Torres group from Salta, Argentina
Formation: No hands, free form
Meter: 3/4
Mood: Dance of liberation, freedom, Magnificence, worship, El Pastor is the Shepherd.
Jim Gold Youtube video: *https://www.youtube.com/watch?v=AfDkK1uUbGs*
Introduction: 3 measures (on 3rd meas draw arms up to T position)
Measures:

FIRST STEP 1

Walk CCW 6 steps

1	Arms T position, R (ct 1), L (ct 2), R (ct 3)
2	L (ct 1), R (ct 2), L (ct 3)

Turn CCW

3	R (ct 1), L (ct 2), R (ct 3)

2 crossing steps, face fwd, arms move down to V position

4	Cross L over R, cross L arm over body (ct 1)
	Step on R in place (ct 2), step L next to R (ct 3)
5	Cross R over L (ct 1), cross R arm over body, step L in place (ct 2), step R next to L (ct 3)

Into ctr

6	Step fwd on L ctr (ct 1). fwd on R (ct 2), fwd on L (ct 3)
	Arms moving fwd and up, palms face fwd and open, eyes look upward twd sky

Crossing step

7	Arms in T, cross R over L (ct 1), step L in place (ct 2), step R next to L (ct 3)

Moving back

8	Step back on L (ct 1), back on R (ct 2), back on L (ct 3), arms coming down top V position Crossing step
9	Arms V position. Step R next to L (ct 1), cross L over R (ct 2), step R in place (ct 3).

Draw step

10	Step on L (ct 1), draw R to L, draw arms up to T (ct 2), hold (ct 3)
11	Hold (ct 1-3)

Repeat Step 1 11x

Prelude to ending (long falsetto note)
8-measure FIRST STEP
1-8   Repeat meas 1-8 of FIRST STEP (While singer holds high falsetto note)

Ending
1   R (ct 1), L (ct 2), R (ct 3)
2   L (ct 1), R (ct 2), L (ct 3)
        Turn CCW:
3   R (ct 1), L (ct 2), R (ct 3)
        1 crossing step, face fwd, arms moving down to V position
4   Cross L over R, swing, cross L arm over body (ct 1)
        Step on R in place (ct 2), step L next to R (ct 3)
5   Step fwd on R (ct 1), bring lft next to R(ct 2-3)
6   Hold in place (ct 1-3)

El Pastor

The shepherd goes with his flock: *Va el pastor con su rebaño*
At the break of dawn: *Al despuntar la manaña*
Going down through the path: *Bajando por el sendero*
From the mountains to the meadow: *De la sierra a la pradera*

He goes mumbing his complaints: *Va musitando sus quejas*
With his little flute: *Con su flautín de carrizo*
Followed by his sheep: *Seguido por sus ovejas*
As if it were a spell: *Como si fuera un hechizo*

The little flute: *El flautín*
Of the shepherd: *Del pastor*
Ay ay ay. . . : *Ay, ay, ay*
Sings this way. . . : *Canta así*

The shepherd is going back: *El pastor ya va de vuelta*
Then the sun is hiding: *Pués el sol se está ocultando*
He is going up through the slope: *Va subiendo por la cuesta*
To keep watch over his flock: *Para guardar su rebaño*

With his flute he goes calling: *Con su flautín va llamando*
One by one his sheep: *Una a una sus ovejas*
And he is communicating to them: *Y les va comunicando*
His joys and sorrows: *Sus goces y sus tristezas*

The little flute. . . : *El flautín*
Of the shepherd. . . : *Del pastor*
Ay ay ay. . . : *Ay, ay, ay*
Sings this way: *Canta así*

ELA APOPSE (GREECE)

Dance Meaning: Come Tonight
Pronunciation: Ela Apopse
Choreography: By Jim Gold in Anatolian/Greek folk dance style
Music: Rebetika: songs of the Heart
Formation: Line
Mood/Feeling: Heavy, earthy, large (steps), open. Hands in W position
Meter: 9/8, slow/slow/slow/ quick/quick/quick: s, s, s, q q q
Jim Gold YouTube video: *https://www.youtube.com/watch?v=lms79ItLgZo*
Introduction: 4 measures
Measures:

FIRST STEP
Moving to the rt

1   Step on R to rt (s), step L behind R (s), step on R to rt (s)
     Step on L in front of R to rt (q), step on R in place (q)
     Step on L in place (q)

(2-6) Repeat meas 1 5x

SECOND STEP
Move into ctr

1   Step fwd on R (s), step fwd on L (s), step fwd on R (s)
     Step fwd on L, lean fwd (q), tap R heel behind L (q), tap R
     heel behind L (q)

Move out of ctr:

2   Step back on R (s), step back on L (s), step back on R (s)
     Step back on L, lean back (s),
     Tap R toe in front of L (q), tap R toe in front of L (q)

3-6 Repeat meas 1-2 2x

ORDER OF STEPS
1. First Step: 6x, Second Step: 3x
2. First Step: 4x, Second Step: 2x
3. First Step: 4x, Second Step: 3x
4. First Step: 6x, Second Step: 2x
5. First Step: 3x Second Step 2x
6. First Step 3x.

Finale: End with R toe tch fwd.

FEST NOZ QUIMPER (BRITTANY, FRANCE)

Dance Meaning: Festival Night (in) Quimper
Pronunciation: Fest Noz Kimper
Choreography: By Jim Gold in Breton folk dance style
Music: Recorded live by Jim Gold at Fest Noz Folk Festival in Quimper July, 2016
Formation: Open circle (closed if enough people) arms swing fwd and bck
Meter: 3/8
Style: Pinky or hand hold, forearms parallel to floor, moving fwd and back
Jim Gold YouTube video: *https://www.youtube.com/watch?v=z3EPSQZ4Fgk*
Introduction: At sound of bombard, wait 4 measures
Measures:

FIRST STEP
Three's (Trois)

1	Step L to left (ct 1), step R next to L (ct 2)
2	Step L to left (ct 1), step R next to L (ct 2)
3	Step R to rt (ct 1), step L next to R (ct 2)
4-12	Repeat meas 1-3 3x

SECOND STEP
Two's (deux)

1	Step L to left (ct 1), step R next to L (ct 2)
2	Step L to left (ct 1), step R next to L (ct 2)
3	Step R to rt (ct 1), step L next to R (ct 2)
4	Step R to rt (ct 1), step L next to R (ct 2)
5-16	Repeat meas 1-4 3x

THIRD STEP
One (un)

1	Step L to left (ct 1), step R next to L (ct 2)
2	Step R to rt (ct 1), step L next to R (ct 2)

Turn CCW (to left) in place in four steps

3	Step L (ct 1), R (ct 2)
4	Step L (ct 1), step R (ct 2)

ORDER OF STEPS
1. First Step: 1x, Second Step: 1x, Third Step: 1x

The Bombard

The *bombard* (Breton, Fr. *bombarde*) is a conical-bore double-reed instrument similar to the oboe, and, like an oboe, it uses reeds made of cane.

In its most primitive form, the bombard has six open holes and possibly a seventh that is often closed with a key. It has a range of just over an octave. Bombards come in a number of keys, based on region or intended use. B-flat is a popular choice for those playing in a Bagad alongside the *binioù braz* (Scottish Highland pipes). In the contemporary setting, bombards may also have complex simple system key-work enabling significant chromatic possibilities. In Breton, the bombard is also known as the *talabard*, and a bombard player as a *talabarder*.

FILLE DELAISSE (NOVA SCOTIA, CANADA)

Dance Meaning: Lost Girl
Pronunciation: Fee De-lass-ei
Choreography: By Jim Gold using folk dance elements from Cajun/French
        Canadian and Bulgarian folk dance style
Styling: Optional clogging: stamp/brush step on off-beats
Music: Barachois
Formation: Open Circle, arms in V position
Notes and comments: Extra beats, and even measures appear periodically in this
        piece. Make the proper timing adjustments.
Meter: 2/4 (4/4)
Jim Gold YouTube video: *https://www.youtube.com/watch?v=np4pzBBioR0*
Introduction: 16 measures
Measures:

FIRST STEP
Walking 12 steps to the right, CCW:

1	R (ct 1), L (ct 2)
2-6	Repeat measure 1 5x
7	Stamp R ft (ct 1,2)
8-14	Repeat meas 1-7

SECOND STEP
7 crossing steps: Moving CCW

1	Cross R over L (ct 1), stamp/brush on L (ct &) step on L (ct 2), stamp/brush on R (ct &)
2	Cross R over L (ct 1), stamp/brush on L (ct &) step on L (ct 2), stamp/brush on R (ct &)
3	Cross R over L (ct 1), stamp/brush on L (ct &) step on L (ct 2), stamp/brush on R (ct &)
4	Cross R over L (ct 1), stamp/brush on L (ct &) step on L (ct 2), stamp/brush on R (ct &)
5	Cross R over L (ct 1), stamp/brush on L (ct &) step on L (ct 2), stamp/brush on R (ct &)
6	Cross R over L (ct 1), stamp/brush on L (ct &) step on L (ct 2), stamp/brush on R (ct &)
7	Step on R (ct 1), lift stiff-legged L preparing to change directions (ct 2)
8-13	Repeat meas 1-6 opp ft in opp dir

14   Step on L (ct 1), step on R in place (ct 2).
          Repeat First and Second Step

THIRD STEP

Walk 8 steps to the right, CCW

1   R (ct 1), L (ct 2)

2-4   Repeat meas 1 3x

4 clog shuffles

5   Brush R toe forward (ct ½ &)
         Brush R toe back (ct ½ &), step on R ft (ct 1)
         Brush L toe forward (ct ½ &)
         Brush L toe back (ct ½ &), step on L ft (ct 2)

6   Repeat meas 5

7-8   Walk bkwd 4 steps: R (ct 1), L (ct 2)
         R (ct 3), L (ct 4)

FOURTH STEP

1-4   Crossing Step: Repeat meas 1-4 of Second Step
         (4x in each direction)

5-8   Repeat meas 1-4 opp ft in opp dir.

ORDER OF STEPS:

1, 2, 1, 2, 3, 4; 1, 2, 3, 4, 3, 4
At slow interlude: 6 slow walking steps,
point R (ct 1,2); then 14 fast walking steps.

FREDO (FRANCE)

Dance Meaning: Fredo: a name
Choreography: by Jim Gold
Music: Le Canard Bleu
Song written by Bernard Dimey
Formation: Open circle, hands in V position
YouTube link: *http://bit.ly/2lb90Rs*
Meter: 3/8
Introduction: 3 meas On measure 4: Step L to lft (ct 1), draw R toe next to L (ct 2-3)
Measures:

FIRST STEP
8 Walking two-step in CCW direction, holding hands behind back

1	R (ct 1), L behind R (ct 2), R in place (ct 3)
2	L (ct 1), R behind L (ct 2), R in place (ct 3)
3-8	Repeat meas 1-2 3x

SECOND STEP
3 Limping step: CCW

1	R (ct 1-2), L (ct 3)
2-3	Repeat meas 1 2x
4	Stop: step on R (ct 1-3)

THIRD STEP
Cherkesia 7, lift, stamp/place

1	L (ct 1), cross R in front of L (ct 2), step L in place (ct 3)
2	Step R in place (ct 1), cross L front of R (ct 2), R in place (ct 3)
3	Step on L (ct 1), lift R (ct 2) , stamp R heel fwd (ct -3)
4	Place R to rt diag rt (ct1-3)

FOURTH STEP
Fwd and back

1	Fwd on R (ct 1), step L next to R (ct 2), R in place (ct 3)
2	Back on L (ct 1), step R next to L (ct 2), L in place (ct 3)
3	Repeat meas 1
4	Back on L (ct 1), step R next to L (ct 2-3)

FIFTH STEP

    Limping step CW

1   L (ct 1-2), R (ct 3)

2-3   Repeat meas 1 2x

4   Step on L (ct 1) draw left and tch L toe next to R (ct 2-3)

SIXTH STEP

    Fwd and back

1   R fwd (ct 1), L next to R (ct 2), R in place (ct 3)

2   L back (ct 1), R next to L (ct 2), L in place (ct 3)

3   R fwd (ct 1), L next to R (ct 2), R in place (ct 3)

4   L back (ct 1), tch R toe next to L (ct 2-3)

SEVENTH STEP

    Rock, lift, stamp/place

1   Rock rt (ct 1-3),

2   Rock left (ct 1), step R next to L (ct 2-3)

3   Step fwd on L (ct 1), lift R (ct 2-3)

3   Stamp R heel fwd (ct 1), place R to rt diag rt (ct 2-3)

    Interlude

1   R fwd (ct 1), L next to R (ct 2), R in place (ct 3)

2   L back (ct 1), draw R toe to L (ct 2-3)

ORDER OF STEPS

1. First (1x), Second(1x), Third(1x), Fourth(1x), Fifth(1x, Sixth(1x)

2-4. Repeat order 3x

    Ending: FIFTH STEP (PART V)

    Fwd and back

       1   R fwd (ct 1), L next to R (ct 2), R in place (ct 3)

       2   L back (ct 1), R next to L (ct 2), L in place (ct 3)

       3   R fwd (ct 1), L next to R (ct 2), R in place (ct 3)

       4   L back (ct 1), tch R toe next to L (ct 2-3)

Fredo

(par Bernard Dimey)

On l' connait d'puis la communale
Le gars qu'est là sur la photo
A la premièr' pag' du journal
Mais on l' reverra pas d' sitôt
Il a saigné deux vieill's mémères
Et buté trois flics,des costauds
Certain'ment sur un coup d' colère
Vu qu'il est pas méchant Frédo
Il a pillé la Banqu' de France
Pour rendr' service à des copains
Pour améliorer leurs finances
Faut bien qu' tout l' mond' y gagn' son pain
Y'a deux trois employés d' la banque
Qu'ont pris d' la mitraill' plein la peau
Bon dieu dans ces cas là on s' planque
Mais c'est pas sa faute à Frédo

Il a liquidé sa frangin'
Un' salop' une rien du tout
Parc' qu'il voulait plus qu'ell' tapine
Elle a calanché sur le coup
Ca c'est des histoir's de famille
Ca regarde pas l' populo
Et puis c'était jamais qu'un' fille
A part ça l'est gentil Frédo
Il a vagu'ment fait du chantage
C'était plutôt pour rigoler
Pour avoir l'air d'être à la page
Mais les môm's qu'il a chouravés
Cétait des p'tits morveux d' la haute
Qui bouff'nt du caviar au kilo
Tout pour les uns rien pour les autres
"C'est pas just"' y disait Frédo

Il a fait l' radam chez les Corses
Un soir qu'il avait picolé
Et comm' i' connait pas sa forc'
Les autr's ils ont pas rigolé
Raphael a sorti son lingue

Bref tout l' mond' s'est troué la peau
C'est vraiment une histoir' de dingues
Vu qu' c'est tous des pôt' à Frédo
L'histoir' des deux voyous d' Pigalle
Qu'il a flingué d'un coeur léger
Moitié camés moitié pédales
Il fallait bien les corriger
Sinon peu à peu qu'est c' qui s' passe
Un jour ça s'allonge aux perdreaux
Total qui c'est qui paie la casse
"C'est nos zigues "y disait Frédo

Un coup d' piqu' feu dans l' péritoine
Et Frédo s'est r'trouvé comm' ça
Le cul sur l'Faubourg saint Antoine
Qu'est c' qu'il foutait dans c' quartier là
Bien sûr il s'est r'trouvé tout d' suite
Avec les poulets sur le dos
Maint'nant vous connaissez la suite
Vous l'avez lue dans les journaux
Un garçon qu'avait tout pour faire
Impeccable mentalité
Délicat , correc' en affaires
Bref il avait qu' des qualités
Ca fait mal quand on l'imagine
En train d' basculer sous l' couteau
De leur salop'rie d' guillotine
Un mec aussi gentil qu' Frédo.

FREILACH (YIDDISH)

Dance Meaning: Happy
Pronunciation: FREY-lak
Choreography: By Jim Gold in Klezmer folk dance style
Style: Romanian and Klezmer style
Music: Luminescent Orchestrii
Formation: Open circle
Meter: 2/4 (4/4)
Jim Gold YouTube video: *https://www.youtube.com/watch?v=3gi9vWhE1-0*
Introduction: 32 measures (Based on 2/4 meter)
Measures:

FIRST STEP
Eight sides to right, CCW

1	R (ct 1), L behind (ct 2)
2	Repeat meas 1
3	Repeat meas 1
4	Repeat meas 1

Cherkassia step: 7 in place

5-8   Cross R over L (ct 1), step on L (ct 2)
Step on R in place (ct 1), step on L in place (ct 2)
Cross R over L (ct 1), step on L (ct 2)
Step on R in place (ct 1)
Stamp L next to R while shouting "Hey!" (ct 2)

9-12   Repeat meas 1-4 opp ft and opp dir
13-16 Repeat meas 5-8 opp ft

SECOND STEP
Into ctr.

1	R (ct 1), L (ct 2)
2	R (ct 1), hop on R, lift L (ct 2)
3-4	Back out: Repeat meas 1-2 opp ft and opp dir

2 grapevine to left

5	R in front (ct 1), L to left side (ct 2)
6	R behind (ct 1), L to left side (ct 2)
7-8	Repeat meas 5-6
9-16	Repeat meas 1-8
17-24	Repeat meas 1-8
25-28	Repeat meas 1-4

2 double time grapevines

29   R in front (ct 1), L to left side (ct &)

       R behind (ct 2), L to left side (ct &)

30   R in front (ct 1), L to left side (ct &)

       R behind (ct 2), L to left side (ct &)

1 grapevine

31   R in front (ct 1), L to left side (ct 2)

32   R behind (ct 1), L to left side (ct 2)

ORDER OF STEPS

1: 2x, 2: 4x, 1: 3x, 2:4x, 1:2x

GORNO ORYAHOVSKO PRAVO HORO (Bulgaria)

Dance Meaning: Gorno Oryahovsko straight hora

Pronunciation: gOrno-orYAhovsko-prAvo-horO. Gorno-Oryahovsko Pravo Horo is named after a town, a town near Veliko Turnovo (NE) called Gorna Oryahovitsa. "Gorno-oryahovsko" is an adjective describing the Horo. "Pravo" means "Straight."

Choreography: Jim Gold in Bulgarian folk dance style

Music: Bulgarian Folk Dances and Songs: Bulgarian National Radio Folk Orchestra, Hristofor Radanov, Conductor

Formation: Open circle leads to the right (counter clockwise)

Handhold: Arms down in V position

Meter: 2/4, 4/4 or 6/8 (counted 123,123)

Jim Gold YouTube video: *http://bit.ly/2lSbplD*

Introduction: 16 measures: Sway to rt and lft

Measures:

FIRST STEP
Basic pravo and sway
Moving Diag rt ctr and diag rt back

1   Step diag fwd on R (ct 1), step lft next to R (ct 2)
2   fwd on R (ct 1-2)
3   Step fwd on L (ct 1-2)
4   Step diag back on R (ct 1), step lft next to R (ct 2)
5   Step back on R (ct 1-2)
6   Step back on L (ct 2)
7   Sway rt (ct 1-2)
8   Sway lft (ct 1-2)

SECOND STEP (Video: Hands on hips)
Crosses and lifts

1   Cross R over L (ct 1), step on L in place (ct 2)
2   step R in place (ct 1), lift L (ct 2)
3   Step on L (ct 1), lift R (ct 2)
4   Step on R in place (ct 1), step on L in place (ct 2)

THIRD STEP (Video: Hands down, V position)
Grapevine 8, 2 lifts, 4 twists, and Second Step
Grapevine 8 CCW

1   Step R to rt (ct 1), step L in front of R (ct 2)

2	step R to rt (ct 1), step L behind R (ct 2)
3	Step R to rt (ct 1), step L in front of R (ct 2)
4	step R to rt (ct 1), step L behind R (ct 2)
	2 lifts, 4 twists
5	Step on R (ct 1), lift L (ct 2)
6	Step on L (ct 1), lift L (ct 2)
7	4 twists: Twist heels to the rt (ct 1), lft (ct 2)
8	rt (ct 1), lft (ct 2)
9-16	**Repeat Second Step 2x**

ORDER OF STEPS

1. First Step: 2x, Second Step: 8x
2. First Step: 2x Second Step: 8x
3. Third Step: On to end: 7x

       Note in Third Step: 3 time: Second Step danced 3x

GRANDFATHER'S CLOCK (USA)

Music: Triple Play All Stars bluegrass group with Drew Smith (Autoharp), Robbie Wedeen (Guitar), and Rich Rainey (Banjo)
Choreography: In bluegrass country dance style by Jim Gold
Formation: Open circle
Meter: 4/4
Jim Gold YouTube video: *https://www.youtube.com/watch?v=JONOo_n7O_c*
Introduction: 8 measures
Measures:

FIRST STEP

8 Clog lifts

1   Step R (ct 1), lift L (ct 2), slight chug back on R (ct 3), slight chug fwd on R (ct 4)

2   Repeat meas 1 opp ft

3-4 Repeat meas 1-2

5-8 Repeat meas 1-4

4 bas de bas

5   Step R (ct 1), cross L over R (ct 2), step on R (ct 3-4)

6   Step L (ct 1), cross R over L (ct 2), step L (ct 3-4)

7-8 Repeat meas 5-6

2 push-steps lft

9   Step "fall" on R and push L to lft side (ct 1-2), step on L (ct 3-4)

10   Step "fall" on R (ct 1-2), step on R (3-4)

4 push-steps rt

11   Push R to rt side (ct 1), step on R (ct 2), step "fall" on L
     Push R to rt side (ct 3), step on R (ct 4)

12   Step "fall" on L and push R to rt side (ct 1), step on R (ct 2)
     step "fall" on L (ct 3), tch R next to L (ct 4)

SECOND STEP

Texas two-step: Walking LOD

1   Step R (ct 1), step L (ct 2), step R (ct 3)
     step L behind R (ct &), step R in place (ct 4)

2   Step L (ct 1), step R (ct 2), step L (ct 3)
     step R behind L (ct &), step L in place (ct 4)

3-8 Repeat meas 1 of SECOND STEP 3x

9   "Stopped short" step on R fwd/stop (ct 1-2)
     "Stopped short" step on R diag rt/stop (ct 3-4)

6 Pas de bas

11   Step R (ct 1), cross L over R (ct 3), step on R (ct 3-4)

12   Step L (ct 1), cross R over L (ct 2), step L (ct 3-4)

13-16 Repeat meas 11-12 2x

THIRD STEP

Transition "Tick tock" step
2 clog lifts.

1   Step R (ct 1), lift L (ct 2),
     slight chug back on R (ct 3), slight chug fwd on R (ct 4)

2   Repeat meas 1 opp ft
     "Tick tock" step:
     Tch R heel fwd (ct 1), tch R heel diag rt (ct 2)
     tap R heel fwd (ct 3), tap R heel diag rt (ct 4)

5-8   Repeat meas 1-4

5-12   Repeat meas 5-12 of FIRST STEP

Ending

1-2   Repeat clog lift from FIRST STEP

3   Tch R heel fwd (ct 1), tch R heel diag rt (ct 2)

4   Tap R heel fwd (ct 1-2)

ORDER OF STEPS

1. First Step: 1x Second Step: 1x, Third Step: 1x

GRKINJA (SERBIA)

Dance Meaning: Greek Girl
Pronunciation: Gurkinya
Choreography: by Jim Gold in Greek folk dance (Hasapico) style
Music: by Serbian singer Željko Samardžić (see his bio below). Borko was our bus driver on the Jim Gold Balkan Splendor 2017 tour of Serbia, Bosnia/Herzegovina, Croatia, and Montenegro.
Formation: Open circle with leader "Hasapico style". Arms: W position
Meter: 2/4
Jim Gold YouTube video: https://www.youtube.com/watch?v=v_hdHS_Jy4M
Jim Gold/ Teaneck Senior Show: *ttps://www.youtube.com/watch?v=mbLTE05mJtk*

Introduction: 8 meas
1   Step R to rt (ct 1-2)
2   Close L to R (ct 1-2)
3   Step R to rt (ct 1-2)
4   Close L to R (ct 1-2)
5   Step L to lft (ct 1-2)
6   Close R to L (ct 1-2)
7   Step L to lft (ct 1-2)
8   Close R to L (ct 1-2)
9   Step R to rt (ct 1-2)
10   Close L to R (ct 1-2)
11   Step L to lft (ct 1-2)
12   Step back on R (ct 1), lift L (ct 2)

FIRST STEP
        Hasapico step
1   Step fwd on L (ct 1), tap R toe behind L (ct 2)
2   Lift R (ct 1), slight kick down/up on R (ct 2)
3   Step R behind L (ct 1) lift L, slight kick down/up (ct 2)
4   Step L behind R (ct 1), lift R (ct 2)
5   Walk CW R (ct 1), L (ct 2)
6   Step back on R (ct 1), lift/swing L across R shin (ct 2)
        2 left heel touches
7   Tch L heel no wt (ct 1-2)
8   Repeat meas 7
9-16   Repeat meas 1-8
        3 left heel touches

17	Tch L heel no wt (ct 1-2)
18-19	Repeat meas 17 2x
20	Step on L (ct 1), lift R (ct 2)

SECOND STEP

Grapevine 7 CW.

1	Cross R over L (ct 1), step L (ct 2)
2	Step R behind L (ct 1), step L (ct 2)
3	Cross R over L (ct 1), step L (ct 2)
4	Step R behind L (ct 1), lift/swing L across R shin (ct 2)

Grapevine 7 CCW

5-7	Repeat steps 1-3 opp dir, opp ft
8	Step on L (ct 1-2)

Into ctr: heavy

9	Step fwd on R (ct 1-2)
10	Step L fwd (ct 1-2)
11	Step fwd R (ct 1), fwd L (ct 2)
12	Step fwd R (ct 1-2)

2 rocks

13	Rock back on L (ct 1-2)
14	Rock fwd on R (ct 1-2)
15	Step back: L (ct 1), R (ct 2)
16	Step back L (ct 1-2)
17-32	Repeat meas 1-16

THIRD STEP

Hora. touches, 7 hora steps

1	Step R to rt (ct 1), step L in front of R (ct 2)
2	Step on R (ct 1), tch L (ct 2)
3	Step on L (ct 1), tch R (ct 2)
4-9	Repeat meas 1-3 3x

Fast hora: Lifts (or two-steps)

10	Step R to rt (ct 1), step L in front of R (ct 2)
11	Step on R (ct 1), lift L (ct 2)
12	Step on L (ct 1), lift R (ct 2)
13-18	Repeat meas 10-12 2x
19	Step R to rt (ct 1), step L in front of R (ct 2)
20	Step on R (ct 1), lift L (ct 2) and **hold**
21	Step on L (ct 1) and **hold**

Fast hora

1-18 Repeat meas 1-3 6x with medium lifts

19-22 **Slow hora and "holds"**

Step on R (ct 1), cross L over R (ct 2),

Step on R and lift L (hold), step on L (ct 1), tch R fwd (ct 2),

lift R (hold)

23-38 Repeat meas 1-15

ORDER OF STEPS

1. First Step: 1x, Second Step: 1x, Third Step
2. First Step: 1x, Second Step: 1x, Third Step

Ending:

22   Step R to rt(ct 1), step L in front of R (ct 2)

23   Step on R (ct 1), lift L (ct 2) and hold

24   Step on L, lift R hold

Ending: step fwd on R

GRKINJA

(Words in Serbian)

Sam sam u tuđem gradu
sa čašom vina k'o s drugom
buzuki s pesmom starom
a ja sa svojom tugom

Ref.
Sirtaki je igrala jedna lepa Grkinja
krišom mi se smešila
a tuga je nestala
Sve što sam joj reći hteo
buzuki je rek'o njoj
a usne su šaputale sagapo, sagapo
Ponoć je u Solunu
osećam dah proleća
noćas se srcu mome
smešila opet sreća

About Željko Samardžić

Željko Samardžić was born in Mostar, at the time part of SR Bosnia and Herzegovina, in Yugoslavia. His father was an ethnic Serb from Montenegro, and his mother Nada was Herzegovinian Serb from the Ilići suburb of Mostar. Samardžić's father was a Yugoslav People's Army officer, which meant that the family had to move around a lot.

After spending the first seven years of his life in Mostar, young Željko lived and attended school in Nikšić, Igalo, and Zadar before eventually returning to Mostar during his teenage years. He first started singing during high school, and soon became known around Mostar for being a good Kemal Monteno impersonator. Samardžić's musical activity during this period was essentially little more than a hobby as he did not put out any official releases and mostly sang in kafanas and restaurants in addition to competing in the occasional obscure festival. The closest he came to wide mainstream success was a schlager "Moja Marija je drugačija" that became a hit in Bosnia during the 1970s after he performed it at *Prvi aplauz* festival in Banja Luka, but he mostly earned his living running a cafe in Mostar, located in close proximity to the famous Old Bridge.

When the Bosnian War broke out in 1992, Željko was wounded in Mostar while sitting in his apartment while chaotic fighting was raging outside. A stray bullet entered his leg and exited his hip. After much trouble, along with his wife and their daughter, he managed to flee the city through the Croat-controlled western part of Herzegovina and eventually reach Serbia after going through Istria, Slovenia and Hungary. Once in Serbia, they lived in the Belgrade suburb of Borča and Samardžić soon started getting low-paying gigs in various discothèques and cafés, building up a fairly devoted niche audience. Almost 40 years old at this point, his big break came unexpectedly when some businessmen who enjoyed his nightclub performances brought him to the elite club Ambassador and also financed him with DM30,000 to record an album with Marina Tucaković and Aleksandar "Futa" Radulović. In 1995, he also appeared at the Pjesma Mediterana festival in Budva, where he left a great impression singing "Sipajte mi još jedan viski "which further opened the doors to show business.

HADI YÜRÜ YÜRÜ (Turkey)

Dance Meaning: Let's go, go, go
Pronunciation: Hai day, yürü, yürü (umlaut pronunciation)
Choreography: By Jim Gold in traditional Turkish folk dance style
Music: Ankarali Namik: Hadi Cikda Gel
Formation: Open Circle, arms down
Jim Gold YouTube video: *https://www.youtube.com/watch?v=5TKczPCm1dE*
Meter: 2/4
Introduction: 4 measures

FIRST STEP

Fwd into ctr, hands in V position

1 Step fwd on R (ct 1), step fwd on L (ct 2)
2 Step in place on R (ct 1), step in place on L (ct &)
Tch R toe to ctr while twisting and lifting hip to left (ct 2)

Back out from ctr. 4 steps

3 Step back on R (ct 1), step back on L (ct 2)
4 Step in place on R (ct 1), step in place on L (ct &)

SECOND STEP

Moving to the right, body facing fwd: hands in W position

1 Step to R (ct 1), cross L over R (ct 2)
2 Step R to right (ct 1), cross L over R (ct &), step R to right side (ct 2)
3-4 Repeat meas 1-2 with opp. ft

"Yemenite" right step

5 Step to right on R (ct 1), step to left on L (ct&)
Cross R over L (ct 2)
6 Step L to left side, drop hands, raise L hand , bring rt hand to left of
face (ct 1), tch R toe to ctr while twisting slightly left, turn/lift R hip
to left, point right hand, palm down twds rt ft (ct 2)

Turning CCW step

7 Step on R as you turn left (ct 1), step on L continue turn (ct 2)
8 Step on R continue turn (ct 1), fact ctr step on L (ct 2).
While turning raise R arm, make CCW circle with R hand.

THIRD STEP

Transition Step, and Halay: Hands in W position

1 Step R to right side (ct 1), bring L tog next to R (ct 2)
Halay

2	Step R to right (ct 1), cross L over R (ct 2)
3	Step R to right (ct 1), lift L (ct 2)
4	Step on L (ct 3), lift R (ct 4)
5-7	Repeat meas 2-4
8-10	Repeat meas 2-4
11-12	Repeat meas 2-3
13	Step on L (ct 1), bring R next to L (ct 2)

FOURTH STEP

Jumps and sevens, hands in V position

1	Facing ctr. Jump to right on R (ct 1), jump to L on L (ct 2)
2	Step to right on R (ct 1), bring L next to R (ct &)
	Step on R (ct 2)

Sevens to the left

3	Step on L (ct 1), bring R next to L (ct &)
	Step on L (ct 2), bring R next to L (ct &)
4	Step on L (ct 1), bring R next to L (ct &)
	Step on L (ct 2)
	Repeat meas 1-2

ORDER OF STEPS

1. First Step: 2x, Second Step: 1x, Third Step: 4x
2. First Step: 2x. Second Step: 1x, Fourth Step: 4x, First Step: 1x. Fourth Step: 1x
3. Third Step: 4x, First Step: 2x, Second Step:1x, Fourth Step: 4x
4. Third Step: 4x, First Step: 2x, Second Step: 1x, Fourth Step: 2x, Second Step: 1x

HASAPICO ARGO (ISORROPIA) (GREECE)

Meaning: Slow balanced hasapico: argo: slow. ισορροπία (isorropia): balance
Pronunciation: Hasapico argo iso rro **pia**
Choreography: Jim Gold in Greek folk dance style
Music: Constantin Paravanos: Greece (Music Around the World)
Formation: Open circle, handds W or V position as indicated
Meter: 2/4
Style: heavy, soulful, cat-like, crouching ready to spring, tension held in body
Jim Gold YouTube video: *http://bit.ly/2pciz66*
Introduction: 4 measures
Measures:

FIRST STEP
Hasapico step
Hands W position, leader T position

1	Step fwd on L (ct 1), tap R toe behind L (ct 2)
2	Lift R (ct 1), slight kick down/up on R (ct 2)
3	Step R behind L (ct 1) lift L, slight kick down/up (ct 2)
4	Step L behind R (ct 1), lift R (ct 2)
5	Walk CW R (ct 1), L (ct 2)
6	Step back on R (ct 1), lift/swing L across R shin (ct 2)
7	Tch L heel no wt (ct 1-2)
8	Repeat meas 7

Fwd and back, leaning fwd, body bent fwd, "hovering" over earth

9	Step fwd on L (ct 1), tap R toe behind L (ct 2)
10	Step back on R (ct 1), lift/swing L across R shin (ct 2)
11	Step fwd on L (ct 1), tap R toe behind L (ct 2)
12	Step back on R (ct 1), step back L (ct 2)

Grapevine 7 CCW

13	Cross R over L (ct 1), step L (ct 2)
14	Step R behind L (ct 1), step L (ct 2)
15	Cross R over L (ct 1), step L (ct 2)
16	Step R behind L (ct 1), lift/swing L across R shin (ct 2)
17-31	Repeat meas 1-15
32	Step R behind L (ct 1), close L to R (ct 2)

SECOND STEP
Hands V position

1	Step R to rt (ct 1), close L to R (ct 2)

2	Step on R (ct 1), tch L ft to rt calve (ct 2)
3	Step L to lft (ct 1-2)
4	Close L to R (ct 1-2)

Two-step in ctr

5	Step fwd on R (ct 1), close L to R (ct 2)
6	Step fwd on R (ct 1-2)
7	Step fwd on L (ct 1) Leader: stay on L, start bringing arms up to T position
8	Step fwd on R (ct 1), swing L across R calve (ct 2). Leader: arms out: T position

Hasapico step

9-12	Step fwd on L (ct 1), tap R toe behind L (ct 2)
2	Lift R (ct 1), slight kick down/up on R (ct 2)
3	Step R behind L (ct 1) lift L, slight kick down/up (ct 2)
4	Step L behind R (ct 1), lift R (ct 2)
5-8	Repeat meas 1-4

7's out moving diag lft

13	Cross R over L (ct 1), step L (ct 2)
14-15	Repeat meas 13 2x
16	Step back on R (ct 1), lift/swing L across R shin (ct 2)

ORDER OF STEPS

1. First Step: 1x, Second Step:2x

HASAPICO ATHENS (GREECE)

Choreography: Jim Gold in Greek folk dance style
Music: Constantin Paravanos: Greece (Music Around the World)
Formation: Open circle. Hand W or V position as indicated
Meter: 2/4
Style: Heavy, soulful, cat-like, crouching ready to spring, tension held in body.
Jim Gold YouTube video: *http://bit.ly/2nBtG9I*
Introduction: 4 measures
Measures:

FIRST STEP
Hasapico step
Leader: Arms out: T position

1	Step fwd on L (ct 1), tap R toe behind L (ct 2)
2	Lift R (ct 1), slight kick down/up on R (ct 2)
3	Step R behind L (ct 1) lift L, slight kick down/up (ct 2)
4	Step L behind R (ct 1), lift R (ct 2)
5	Walk CW R (ct 1), L (ct 2)
6	Step back on R (ct 1), lift/swing L across R shin (ct 2)
7	Tch L heel no wt (ct 1-2)
8	Repeat meas 7

Fwd and back, leaning fwd, body bent fwd, "hovering" over earth

9	Step fwd on L (ct 1), tap R toe behind L (ct 2)
10	Step back on R (ct 1), lift/swing L across R shin (ct 2)
11	Step fwd on L (ct 1), tap R toe behind L (ct 2)
12	Step back on R (ct 1), step back L (ct 2)

Grapevine 7 CCW

13	Cross R over L (ct 1), step L (ct 2)
14	Step R behind L (ct 1), step L (ct 2)
15	Cross R over L (ct 1), step L (ct 2)
16	Step R behind L (ct 1), lift/swing L across R shin (ct 2)
17-31	Repeat meas 1-15
32	Step R behind L (ct 1), close L to R (ct 2)

SECOND STEP
Hands in V position

1	Step R to rt (ct 1), close L to R (ct 2)
2	Step on R (ct 1), tch L ft to rt calve (ct 2)
3	Step L to lft (ct 1-2)

4	Close L to R (ct 1-2)
	Two-step in ctr
5	Step fwd on R (ct 1), close L to R (ct 2)
6	Step fwd on R (ct 1-2)
7	Step fwd on L (ct 1)
8	Step fwd on R (ct 1), swing L across R calve (ct 2)
	Hasapico step
9-12	Step fwd on L (ct 1), tap R toe behind L (ct 2)
2	Lift R (ct 1), slight kick down/up on R (ct 2)
3	Step R behind L (ct 1) lift L, slight kick down/up (ct 2)
4	Step L behind R (ct 1), lift R (ct 2)
5-8	Repeat meas 1-4
	7's out moving diag lft
9	Cross R over L (ct 1), step L (ct 2)
10-11	Repeat meas 13 2x
12	Step back on R (ct 1), lift/swing L across R shin (ct 2)

ORDER OF STEPS
1. First Step: 1x, Second Step:1x

HEJ GOROL CI JO GOROL (POLAND)

Choreography: by Jim Gold in South Polish folk dance style
Jim Gold YouTube Video: *https://www.youtube.com/watch?v=2VRYZJjLnMk*
Introduction: 8 measures
Measures:

FIRST STEP
Slow: Cross and slap

1	Step R to rt (ct 1), cross L over R (ct 2)
2	Repeat meas 1
3	Step R to rt (ct 1), slap inside of L boot (ct 2)
4	Step on L (ct 1), slap R knee with back of R hand (ct 2)
5	Make full slow turn: Raise L hand high up, palm facing out of circle, and R hand down with palm facing into circle. Step on R (ct 1), L (ct 2)
6	R (ct 1), step L next to R (ct 2)

SECOND STEP
Faster: Two-and-one csardas and rida: 6 measure section

1	Step R to rt (ct 1), bring L next to R (ct 2)
2	Repeat meas 1
3	Step L to lft (ct 1), tch R next to L (ct 2)
3-6	Repeat meas 1-3

Rida

7	Step R to rt (ct 1) rising on R toes Cross L over R lowering self (coming down) on flat ft (ct 2)
8-9	Repeat meas 7 2x
10-12	Repeat meas 1-3. Into ctr
13	**Rida fwd step** Step R fwd (ct 1), bring L next to R (ct 2)
14	Repeat meas 13
15	Step on R (ct 1), tch L toe next to R (ct 2) Out of ctr
	Rida back step
16	Step back on L (ct 1), bring R next to L (ct 2)
17	Repeat meas 16
18	Step back on L (ct 1), tch R next to L (ct 2)

SECOND STEP

Faster: Two-and-one csardas and rida: 4 measure section

4-measure section is only in first half of dance

1-12   Repeat meas 1-12 of Part I

HONGA (YIDDISH, FROM MOLDAVIA)

Dance Meaning: A dance form from Moldavia
Pronunciation: HON-ga
Choreography: By Jim Gold. Fusion style: Using Klezmer, Croatian, Hungarian, and Moldavian folk dance style.
Music: Itzak Perlman and the Klezmatics
Formation: Open circle, arms in V position
Meter: 2/4 (4/4)
Jim Gold YouTube video: *https://www.youtube.com/watch?v=hv6dOBavAtI*
Introduction: 4 measures
Measures: 2/4

FIRST STEP
        Croatian drmes/csardas step: Drmes body-tremble
1-2   Step R to R (ct 1), step L next to R (ct 2)
        Step R to R (ct 1), touch L next to R (ct 2)
3-4   Repeat step 1-2 opp ft and opp dir
5-8   Repeat meas 1-4

SECOND STEP
        8 syncopated Moldavian
1   In place: Step on R (ct 1), tap L next to R (ct &)
        Lift L (ct 2), tap L (ct &)
2   Repeat meas 1 opp, ft and opp dir.
3-4   Repeat meas 1-2
5-8   Repeat meas 1-4

THIRD STEP
        Box. Facing ctr. moving to R, CCW
1   Step R to right (ct 1), bring L next to R (ct 2)
2-4   Repeat meas 1 3x
        Moving into ctr. 16 quick shuffling steps
5   R (ct 1), L (ct &)
6-8   Repeat meas 5 7x
9   Move to left:
        Cross R over L (ct 1), step on L to L (ct 2)
10-12 Repeat meas 9 3x
        Moving bkwd:
13-16 Step back on R (ct 1-2), back on L (ct 1-2)
Step back on R (ct 1), back on L (ct 2)
Step on R (ct 1-2)

HORA LUI BUDISTEANU (ROMANIA)

Dance Meaning: Budisteanu's Circle Dance
Pronunciation: Hora Loui Budisteanu
Choreography: by Jim Gold in Romania folk dance style
Music: Greetings from Romania: Volume I
Formation: Open circle, hands in W position. On turns go to V position.
Meter: 2/4
Jim Gold YouTube video: *https://www.youtube.com/watch?v=dKjfZk9s5yE*
Introduction: 2 measures
Measures:

FIRST STEP
Grapevine CW and turn CCW

1	Moving CW step R over L (ct 1), step L to lft (ct 2)
2	Step R behind L (ct 1), step L to lft (ct 2)
3-4	Repeat meas 1-2
5-6	Repeat meas 1-2

CCW turn in 4 steps. Arms go to V position

7-8	R (ct 1), L (ct 2,) R (ct 1), L (ct 2)
9-32	Repeat meas 1-8 3x

SECOND STEP
Two-step and grapevine CCW

1	Step R fwd (ct 1), bring L next to R (ct 2)
2	Step on L (ct 1-2)
3-4	Repeat meas 1-2 opp ft

Grapevine CCW

5	Step on R to rt (ct 1), step on L behind rt (ct 2)
6	Step on R to rt (ct 1), step on L in front of R (ct 2)
7-8	Repeat meas 5-6
9-32	Repeat meas 1-8 3x

ORDER OF STEPS
First Step: 1x, Second Step: 1x

HORA LUI GRIGORAS (ROMANIA)

Dance Meaning: George Dinicu's Hora
Pronunciation: Hora Lewi Grigoras Dinicu
Choreography: by Jim Gold in Romanian folk dance style
Music: Greetings from Romania: Volume I
Formation: Line, hands in W position
Meter: 4/4
Jim Gold YouTube video: *https://www.youtube.com/watch?v=2U88VAKyRPI*
Introduction: 8 measures
Measures:

FIRST STEP

Moving diag right and diag back

1	Move diag fwd: R (ct 1), L (ct 2), R (ct 3), tch L (ct 4)
2	Move diag back: L (ct 1), R (ct 2), L (ct 3), tch R (ct 4)
3-4	Repeat meas 1-2

Face ctr. Move to rt

5	R (ct 1), L behind R (ct 2)
	R (ct 3), stamp L next to R (ct 4)
6	Repeat meas 5 opp ft opp dir
7-8	Repeat meas 5-6

SECOND STEP

Crossing steps 16: Cherkassia

1	Step R to rt (ct 1), cross L in front of R (ct 2)
	Step R in place (ct 3), step L next to R (ct 4)
2	Cross R over L (ct 1), step L in place (ct 2)
	Step R next to L (ct 3), cross L over R (ct 4)
3	Step R in place (ct 1), step L next to R (ct 2)
	Cross R over L (ct 3), step L in place (ct 4)
4	Repeat meas 1

Sides:7

5	Ste R to rt (ct 1), step L behind R (ct 2)
	Step R to rt (ct 3), step L behind R (ct 4)
6	Step R to rt (ct 1), step L behind R (ct 2)
	Step R to rt (ct 3), stamp L next to R (ct 4)
7-8	Repeat meas 6 opp ft opp dir

SECOND STEP VARIATION

1   Step R to rt (ct 1), cross L in front of R (ct 2)
        Step R in place (ct 3), step L next to R (ct 4)

2   Cross R over L (ct 1), step L in place (ct 2)
        Step R next to L (ct 3), cross L over R (ct 4)

3   Step R next to L (ct 1), cross L over R (ct &)
        Step on R in place (ct 2), step L in place (ct &)
        Cross R over L (ct 3), step L in place (ct &)
        Step R next to L (ct 2), cross L over R (ct &)

4   Step R in place (ct 3), step L next to R (ct &)
        Cross R over L (ct 4), step L in place (ct &)

Sides: 7

5   Ste R to rt (ct 1), step L behind R (ct 2)
        Step R to rt (ct 3), step L behind R (ct 4)

6   Step R to rt (ct 1), step L behind R (ct 2)
        Step R to rt (ct 3), stamp L next to R (ct 4)

7-8   Repeat meas 6 opp ft opp dir

ORDER OF STEPS

1. First Step: 1x, Second Step: 1x

HORA YIA TA MATIA POU AGAPO (GREECE)

Dance Meaning: Hora of the Look (Glance) that I Love
Pronunciation: Hora Ya Ta Matya Poo Agapo
Choreography: by Jim Gold in Greek folk dance style
Music: Rebetika: Songs of the Heart
Formation: Open circle, arms in W pos
Meter: 4/4
Jim Gold Youtube video: https://www.youtube.com/watch?v=349s5aeiJwo
Introduction: 4 measures
Measures:

FIRST STEP
Moving CCW
1   Grapevine: R (ct 1), L behind (ct 2), R (ct 3), L in front (ct 4)
2   Lifts: R (ct 1), Lift L(ct 2), Step on L(ct 3), lift R(ct 4)
     Add turns, etc.
3-8   Repeat meas 1-2 3x

SECOND STEP
Into ctr: 3 back pas de bas and stamps
1   Step fwd on R(ct 1), L behind R (ct &), step fwd on R (ct 2)
     Step fwd on L(ct 3), R behind L (ct &), step fwd on L (ct 4)
2   Step fwd on R(ct 1), L behind R (ct &), step fwd on R (ct 2)
     Step on L(ct 3), stamp on R next to L(ct 4)
     Back out of ctr
3   Step back on R (ct 1), lift L(ct 2)
     step back on L(ct 3), lift R (ct 4)
     Walk back 4 steps:
4   R (ct 1),L (ct 2),R (ct 3), L(ct 4)
5   Repeat meas 1
6   Step fwd on R(ct 1), L behind R (ct &), step fwd on R (ct 2)
     Step on L(ct 3), stamp R next to L(ct 4), stamp R again(ct &).
7-8   Repeat meas. 3-4
9-16   Repeat meas 1-8

ORDER OF STEPS:
1. First Step: 1x, Second Step: 1x

ISKAT ME MAMO (BULGARIA)

Dance Meaning: Mother, two men want to marry me.
     (Translation by George Vishegonov and family)
Pronunciation: Eeskot Meh mamo dvama
Choreography: by Jim Gold in Bulgarian folk style
Music: Unknown
Formation: Open circle
Meter: 7/8: slow/quick/quick: s, q, q
Jim Gold YouTube video: *https://www.youtube.com/watch?v=ejBHK_gdg40*
Introduction: 8 measures
Measures: 7/8 time slow/quick/quick: s/q q

FIRST STEP
Facing CCW: **Rocking step**
1   Step fwd on R (ct s), rock back on L (ct q), rock fwd on R (ct q)
    Walk
2   Step L (ct s), step R (q. q)
3-4 Repeat meas 1 using opp ft
    6-step Grapevine:
5   Face fwd: Step R to rt (s), step L behind R (ct q), step R to rt (ct, q)
6   Cross L over R (ct s), step R to rt (ct q), step L behind R (ct q)
    Two lifts
7   Step R (ct s), lift L (ct q. q)
8   Step on L (ct s), lift R (ct q, q)
    Facing fwd:
9   Rock fwd on R (ct s), back on L (ct q), fwd on R (ct q)
    1/4 turn to face CW: Walk
10   Step L (ct s), step R (ct q, q)
11   Step on L (ct s), rock back on R (ct q), fwd on L (ct q)
12   Repeat meas 10 opp ft
    4-step Grapevine
13   Step R front of L (ct s), step L to lft side (ct q), step R behind L (ct q)
14   Step L to lft side(ct s), cross R front of L (ct q), step L in place (ct q)
15   Step on R (ct s), lift L (ct q, q)
16   Step on L (ct s), lift R (ct q, q)
17-24 Repeat meas 1-8

SECOND STEP

           Into ctr

1   R (ct s), L (ct q), R (ct q),

2   L (ct s), R (ct q), L (ct q)

3   Step on R (ct s), cross L over R (ct q), step on R in place (ct q)

4   Step on L (ct s), lift R (ct q, q)

           Back out of ctr

5   R (ct s), L (ct q), R (ct q)

6   L (ct s), R (ct q), L (ct q)

7   Tch right heel diag.to rt (ct s), tch R heel fwd (ct q, q)

8   Tch right heel diag rt (ct s), tch right toe next to lft ft (ct q. q)

ORDER OF STEPS

1. First Step: 1x, Second Step: 1x

I'VE BEEN UP AND DOWN (USA)

Choreography: By Jim Gold in Reggae/American folk dance style
Source: Reggae style
Music: Louie Fleck CD
Formation: Open Circle, individual style, hands free
Meter: 4/4
Jim Gold YouTube video: *https://www.youtube.com/watch?v=nfeyRMPJuJM*
Introduction: 4 measures
Measures:

	Introduction: Start with arms down.
1	Bring arms up as you step forward on R (ct 1)
	Stamp L next to R (ct 2)
	Bring arms down as you step back on L (ct 3)
	Stamp R next to L (ct 4)
2-4	Repeat meas 1

FIRST STEP

1	Step forward on R (ct 1)
	Bring arms up in W position, stamp L next to R (ct 2)
	Step back on L (ct 3)
	Bring arms down in V position, stamp R next to L (ct 4)

8-step grapevine to left: CW

2	Dip slightly as you step on R in front of L (ct 1), step on L next to R (ct &)
	Step on R behind L (ct 2), step on L to left side (ct &)
	Step on R in front of L (ct 3), step on L next to R (ct &)
	Step on R behind L (ct 4), step on L to left side (ct &)
3-8	Repeat meas 1-2 3x

SECOND STEP:

Into ctr. Two 2-steps

1	R (ct 1), L(ct &), R (ct 2) , L (ct 3), R (ct &), L(ct 4)
2	Bend forward as you step forward on R (ct 1)
	Stamp lightly on L in back of R (ct 2)
	Step back on L as you straighten (ct 3)
	Light stamp on R in front of L (ct 4)
3	Step R to right (ct 1), lean hard to right with optional "Uuh!" grunt (ct 2)

Step on L (ct 3), touch R next to L (ct 4)

Shoulder-shimmy back

4 Walk bkwd 4 steps with shoulder shimmy:
    R (ct 1), L (ct 2), R (ct 3), L (ct 4)

5-8 Repeat meas 1-4

ORDER OF STEPS

First Step: 4x, Second Step: 2x, First: 6x, Second: 2x
First: 6x, Second: 2x, First: 6x, Second: 2x, First: 4x
Second: 1x, First: 4x as music fades out

JAUNAS BERNUZELIS (LITHUANIA)

Dance Meaning: Young Lad
Pronunciation: Jawnas Bernu-ZE-lis
Choreography: By Jim Gold in eclectic folk dance style
Formation: Open Circle
YouTube Video: *http://bit.ly/2nSegi7*
YouTube Group Video: *http://bit.ly/2oh9yuB*
Meter: 4/4
Introduction: 6 measures
Measures:

       FIRST STEP
       Into ctr, arms in escort position

1   R (ct 1), L (ct 2), R (ct 3), kick L (ct 4)
       Back out
2   L (ct 1), R (ct 2), L (ct 3), stamp R (ct 4)
3-6   Repeat measures 1-2, 2x

       SECOND STEP
       8 two-steps to the right, CCW: arms in V position

1   R (ct 1), L (ct &), R (ct 2), L (ct 3), R (ct &), L (ct 4)
2-4   Repeat meas 1 3x
       Face ctr, march in place
5   Step R in place (ct 1), step L in place (ct 2)
       Step R in place (ct 3), step L in place (ct 4)
6   Step forward. on R (ct 1), step on L next to R (ct &), step on R in place (ct 2)
       Step back on L (ct 3), step on R next to L (ct 4)

JERUSALEM RIDGE (USA)

Choreography: By Jim Gold in Irish-America folk dance style
Music: Jerusalem Ridge: Mark O'Conner
Formation: Solo dance
Styling: Arms down at sides, Irish dance style.
Notes and comments: Extra beats (counts) appear periodically in this piece. Make the proper timing adjustments during the dance. Meter: 4/4
Jim Gold YouTube video: *https://www.youtube.com/watch?v=hboaMOElrVk*
Introduction: 8 measures
Measures:

FIRST STEP
Into ctr

1   Step forward on R (ct 1)
      Light heel brush-stamp with L (ct &)
      Step forward on L(ct 2)
      Light heel brush-stamp with R (ct &)
      Step on R (ct 3), touch L next to R (ct 4)
      Out of ctr

2   Step back on L (ct 1), back on R (ct 2)
      Back on L (ct 3), touch R next to L (ct 4)

3-4   Repeat meas 1-2

5-8   Repeat meas 1-2 2x

SECOND STEP
12 clog shuffle steps: Starts on the upbeat

1   Brush R toe forward (ct ½ &)
         Brush R toe back (ct ½ &), step on R ft (ct 1)
      Brush L toe forward (ct ½ &)
         Brush L toe back (ct ½ &), step on L ft. (ct 2)
      Brush R toe forward (ct ½ &)
         Brush R toe back (ct ½ &), step on R ft (ct 3)
      Brush L toe forward (ct ½ &)
         Brush L toe back (ct ½ &), step on L ft (ct 4)

2-3   Repeat meas 1 2x
      Complete left turn in 4 steps

4   R (ct 1), L (ct 2), R (ct 3), L (ct 4).

THIRD STEP

Face ctr

1   Touch bottom of R ft to inner calf of L leg (ct 1)

       Push R ft. diag out (ct 2)

       Step on R in place (ct 3)

       Step on L in place (ct &)

       Step on R in place (ct 4)

2   Same as above, opp ft and opp dir

3   Touch R toe behind L (ct 1)

       Brush R ft. to the right (ct 2)

       Brush R ft across in front of L (ct 3)

       Brush R ft to right (ct 4)

7's to the right, CCW

4   Step R to the right (ct 1), L behind R (ct &)

       Step R to the right (ct 2), L behind R (ct &)

       Step R to the right (ct 3), L behind R (ct &)

       Step on R (ct 4)

5-8   Repeat meas 1-4 opp ft and opp dir

JEST VINO (RUSSIA)

Dance Meaning: There is wine
Pronunciation: Jest VI-no
Choreography: By Jim Gold in Russian folk dance style
Music: The Mayan
Formation: Open circle
Meter: 2/4
Jim Gold YouTube video: *https://www.youtube.com/watch?v=7K5JFjB1spI*
Introduction: 8 measures
Measures:

FIRST STEP
Moving CCW

1	Step on R (ct 1), scuff L (ct &), step on L (ct 2), scuff R (ct &)
2	Two-step: R (ct 1), L (ct &), R(ct 2), scuff L (ct &)
3-4	Repeat meas 1-2 opp ft
5	Facing ctr, step R to the right side(ct 1), L behind R (ct &)
	Step on R (ct 2) , tap L heel next to R (ct &)
6	Repeat meas 5 opp ft

Into ctr

7	Repeat meas 1

Run 4 small steps slightly forward, lean slightly forward

8	R (ct 1), L (ct &), R (ct 2), L (ct &)

SECOND STEP
Syncopated step, face ctr

1	Step on R (ct 1), tap L heel to side of R, no weight (ct &)
	Lift L (ct 2), tap L heel in place (ct &)
2	Repeat meas 1 opp ft
3-4	Repeat meas 1-2

Reel back

5	Lift R, hook it behind L (ct 1), step on R (ct &)
	Lift L, hook behind R (ct 2), step on L (ct &)
6	Repeat meas 5
7	Repeat meas 1

In place with light stamps

8	L (ct 1), R (ct &), L (ct 2)

Note: Jest Vino used as a training, practice, or warm-up dance for Oy, Baboushka. The choreography for both dances is the same, only Jest Vino is slower.

KAMENOPOLSKO ORO (Bulgaria)

Dance Meaning: Rocky field
Pronunciation: Kamenopolsko Oro
Choreography: by Jim Gold in north Bulgarian folk dance style.
Music: *Bulgarian Folk Dances* (Folkraft Records, 1159 Broad Street, Newark, NJ
    Supervised and recorded in Bulgaria by Dennis Boxell
Formation: Line
Meter: 2/4
Jim Gold YouTube video: *https://www.youtube.com/watch?v=EfOSkuByFrQ*
Introduction: 8 measures
Measures:

FIRST STEP

Three two-steps into ctr

1	R (ct 1), L (ct &), R (ct 2)
2	L (ct 1), R (ct &), L (ct 2)
3	R (ct 1), L (ct &), R (ct 2)
4	Turn body rightward: stamp on L shouting "Hey!" (ct 1)
	Turn body to face ctr: lift L, shout "Ha!" (ct 2)

Moving backward out of ctr

5	Step on L (ct 1), lift R (ct 2),
6	step on R (ct 1), lift L (ct 2)
7	Step on L (ct 1), step on R next to L (ct 2)
8	Step on L (ct 1), lift R (ct 2)

SECOND STEP

Crossing step

1	Step on R in place (ct 1), cross L over R (ct 2)
2	Step on R in place (ct 1), lift L (ct 2)
3-4	Repeat 1-2 using opp ft
5-6	Repeat meas 1-2. Shout "Asega!" (Now)
5	Step on R in place (ct 1), cross L over R (ct 2)
6	Step on R in place, shout "Ase"
	Lift L, shout "ga" (ct 2)

Fast cross-seven step

7	Step on L in place (ct 1), cross R over L (ct &)
	Step on L in place (ct 2), step on R next to L (ct &)
8	Step on L in place (ct 1), cross R over L (ct &)
	Step on L in place (ct 2)
9-16	Repeat meas 1-8

THIRD STEP

Four grapevines moving to left

1   Cross R over L (ct 1), step L to side of R (ct 2)

2   Cross R behind L (ct 1), step L to side of R (ct 2)

3-4 Repeat meas 1-2

5-6 Repeat meas 1-2

7-8 Repeat meas 1-2: Shout **"Dai go zivo asega!"** (Give it life, now!)

7   Cross R over L (ct 1) shout **"Dai go"**
     Step L to side of R (ct 2) shout **"zivo"**

8   Cross R behind L (ct 1) shout **"ase"**
     Step L to side of R(ct 2)shout **"ga"**

FOURTH STEP

Crossing "two-step: grapevine moving to left

1   Cross R over L (ct 1), step on L in place (ct &)
     Step on R in place (ct 2)

2   Step on L to side of R (ct 1), step on R behind L (ct &)
     Step on L in place (ct 2)

3-4 Repeat meas 1-2

5-6 Repeat meas 1-2

7-8 Repeat meas 1-2

ORDER OF STEPS

First Step: 1x, Second Step: 2x, Third Step: 1x, Fourth Step: 1x
First Step: 2x, Second Step: 2x, Third Step: 1x, Fourth Step: 1x
First Step: 2x, Second Step: 1x, Third Step: 1x, Fourth Step: 1x
First Step: 1x

KAPURA (Slovakia)

Dance Meaning: Threshold. East Slovak dialect. Etymologically, related to word *Prague*, meaning "threshold."
Pronunciation: KA-pu-ra
Music: A Od Presova with Hanka Servicka
Choreography: By Jim Gold using traditional steps from Slovakia
Formation: Open circle
Meter: 4/4
Jim Gold YouTube video: *https://www.youtube.com/watch?v=uKA_XaWYwyE*
Introduction: 4 measure
Measures:

        FIRST STEP
        Slovak Csardas
        Facing ctr, moving right, hands free, right hand held high Slovak
            style.
        Csardas step

1	Step to R (ct 1), bring L next to R (ct 2)
	Step to R (ct 3), bring L next to R (ct 4)
2	Repeat meas 1 in opposite direction
3-8	Repeat meas 1-2 3x

        SECOND STEP
        Csardas into ctr

1	Step into ctr with R (ct 1), step into ctr with L (ct 2)
	Step into ctr with R (ct 3), lift L (ct 4)
2	Out of the ctr: Repeat meas 1 opp ft and opp dir
3-4	Repeat meas 1-2
5	Repeat meas 1. On ct 4, lift L leg slap L boot (L knee for women) with R hand
6	Repeat meas 9 going out of circle. On ct 4. lift R leg, slap R boot (or knee) with R hand
7	Step on R(ct 1), slap left boot (ct 2)
	Step on L (ct 3), slap right boot (ct 4)
8	Step on R foot, clap hands once (ct 1)
	Bring L foot behind R leg and slap L foot (ct 2)
	Step on L (ct 3-4)

THIRD STEP

        8 Rida steps to right, CCW, hold hands, arms in V position

1   Step on R (ct 1), cross L in front of R (ct 2)

       step on R (ct 3), cross L in front of R (ct 4)

2   Step on R (ct 1), cross L in front of R (ct 2)

       Step on R (ct 3), stamp L next to R no weight (ct 4)

3-4   Repeat meas 1-2 opp dir and opp ft

       Repeat First and Second Step

FOURTH STEP

        "Friss" or Fast Slovak Csardas

1-2   Repeat meas 1-2 of FIRST STEP

3-4   Repeat meas 1-2

5-8   Repeat meas 5-8 from Second Step

1-4   Repeat meas 1-4 of Third Step: Rida

5-8   Repeat meas 1-4 of First Step: Slovak Csardas

       Complete 8-step turn to left:

9   Step on R (ct 1), step on L (ct 2)

       Step on R (ct 3), step on L (ct 4)

10   Step on R (ct 1), step on L (ct 2)

       Step on R (ct 3), step on L (ct 4)

       Facing ctr

11   Step to R (ct 1), bring L next to R (ct 2), step to R (ct 3-4)

12   Step on L to left (ct 1-2)

       snap R next to L (ct 3-4)

       Repeat "friss" pattern three times

Dance notes by Jim Gold: Presented by Jim Gold at the Florida Folk Dance Camp, February 2004.

KARAMFILO, FIL-FILO MOME (BULGARIA)

Dance Meaning: My little girl, Carnation
Pronunciation: Karamfilo, Fil-Filo Mome
Choreography: by Jim Gold in Macedonian-Bulgarian folk dance style
Music: Stoyan Djadjef: Makedonski Pesni
Formation: Open Circle, arms in W position
Meter: 7/8: slow/quick/quick: s, q, q
Jim Gold YouTube video: *https://www.youtube.com/watch?v=lI-5rVHsV8Q*
Introduction: 8 measures
Measures:

FIRST STEP

Moving to Rt

1   Step R (s), step L (q), step R (q)
2   Step L (s), step R (q), step L (q)

Crossing step, face ctr

3   Step on R (s), cross L in front of R (q), step on R in place (q)
4   Step on L (s), cross R in front of L (q), step on L in place (q)

Lesnoto step

5   Step on R (s), lift L (q), step on L in front of R (q)
6   Step on R (s), lift L (q, q)
7   Step on L (s), lift R (q, q)

Walk two steps to rt

8   R (s), L (q, q)
9-15 Repeat meas 1-7

Face ctr

16 Step to R (s), place L next to R (q, q)

SECOND STEP

4 measure Patrioti Step

1   Step into ctr. on L (s), lift R in front of L (q, q)
2   In slow swing, bring R in a ronde de jambe behind L (s)
    Place R ft behind L knee (q, q)
3   In a slow swing, bring R leg fwd in front of L (s)
    Place R ft above L knee (q, q)
4   R ankle rests on L knee: Bounce once on L ft (s)
    Bounce twice on L ft (q, q)
5   Step to rt on R ft (s), step L behind R (q, q)
6   Step R to rt (s), place L next to R (q, q)

7-12   Repeat meas 1-6
13-18 Repeat meas 1-6
        Optional: with opp ft or alternate feet

ORDER OF STEPS
1. First Step: 1x, Second Step 1x
2. First Step: 2x, Second Step 1x
3. First Step: 2x, Second Step 1x
4. First Step: 2x, Second Step 1x

KATERINA MOU (GREECE)

Dance Meaning: My Catherine
Pronunciation: Katerina Moo
Choreography: Jim Gold in Greek folk dance style
Music: Constantin Paravanos: Greece (Music Around the World)
Formation: Open circle, hands W or V position as indicated
Meter: 2/4
Style: Up beat, happy, bouncy
Jim Gold YouTube video link: *http://bit.ly/2ovELGE*
Introduction: 2 measures

Intro step: Sides
1. Step R to ft (ct 1), close L to R (ct 2)
2. Repeat meas 1
3. Step L to lft (ct 1), close R to L (ct 2)
4. Repeat meas 3
5-8. Repeat meas 1-4

FIRST STEP
Into ctr and back: Walk proud, joyful, bouncy. Hands in W position
1   Step fwd on R (ct 1), L (ct 2)
2   R (ct 1), tch L heel fwd (ct 2)
3   Step back on L (ct 1), R (ct 2)
4   L (ct 3), tch R heel R fwd (ct 4)
Two steps
5   Step fwd on R (ct 1), bring L next to R (ct &), step on R (ct 2), brush L heel (ct &)
6   Step fwd on L (ct 1), bring R next to L (ct &), step on L (ct 2), brush R heel (ct &)
7   Step back on R (ct 1), bring L next to R (ct &)
     Step back on R (ct 2), brush L heel (ct &)
8   Step back on L(ct 1), step R next to L(ct 2)

SECOND STEP
Sides. Hands in V position
1   Step R to rt (ct 1), step L behind R (ct 2)
2   step R to rt (ct 1), step L behind R (ct 2)
Grapevine 5 and light heel stamps
3   Step R to rt (ct 1), step L front of R (ct &)

Step R to rt (ct 2), step L behind R (ct &)
4   Step on R (ct 1), light stamp with L heel (ct 2)
5-7   Repeat meas 1-4, opp dir, opp ft
8   Step on R (ct 1), tch R toe to L instep (ct 2)

ORDER OF STEPS
1. First Step: 1x, Second Step:1x
2. First Step: 1x, Second Step:1x
        Sides 2x
3. First Step: 1x, Second Step:1x
4. First Step: 1x, Second Step:1x
        Sides 1x
5. First Step: 1x, Second Step:1x
6. First Step: 1x, Second Step:1x

KOMARONI (Yiddish, from Slovakia)

Dance Meaning: Name of town on Danube in Slovakia
Pronunciation: KO-maroni
Choreography: By Jim Gold in Klezmer folk dance style
Music: Carpati: Yale Strom
Commentary: Beautiful accordion playing by Peter Stan, the wonderful clarinet
and sopranino is by Norbert Stachel, superb guitar by Fred Benedetti and
solid bass by Jeff Pekarek. These musicians are all part of Yale Strom &
Hot Pstromi. Wonderful choreography to a Rom folk melody often per
formed by klezmer musicians in Slovakia.
Formation: Open circle. Arms in W position
Meter: 4/4
Jim Gold YouTube video: *https://www.youtube.com/watch?v=p3aldgjrxII*
Introduction: 4 measures
Measures:

FIRST STEP
Moving into ctr, diagonally rightward

1   2 two-steps: R (ct 1), L (ct &), R (ct 2) , L (ct 3), R (ct &),
L (ct 4)

2 lift steps

2   Step on R (ct 1), lift L (ct 2), step L (ct 3), lift R (ct 4)

Moving out of ctr, diagonally rightward

3   R (ct 1), L (ct 2), R (ct 3), L (ct 4)

2 Lifts steps

4   Step on R (ct 1), lift L (ct 2), step L (ct 3), lift R (ct 4)

Moving straight into ctr

5   2 two-steps: R (ct 1), L (ct &), R (ct 2), L (ct 3), R (ct &), L (ct 4)

2 lift steps

6   Step on R (ct 1), lift L (ct 2), step L (ct 3), lift R (ct 4)

Moving out of ctr

7   R over L (ct 1), step on L (ct 2). R over L(ct 3), step on L(ct 4)

Continue out of circle with a 3-step grapevine

8   Cross R over L (ct 1), step on L in place (ct 2)
Step on R next to L (ct 3), step on L in place (ct 4)

SECOND STEP
Grapevine to the left CW

9   Cross R over L (ct 1), step on L to side of R (ct 2)

Step on R behind L(ct 3), step on L to side of R(ct 4)

10   Repeat meas 9

11   Step on R(ct 1), lift L (ct 2), step on L in place(ct 3), kick and
      point R ft fwd 4)

      Gypsy turn

12   Put R heel on floor in front of L ft, turn slowly left (ct 1-4)

KOTLENSKA SVATBARSKA RUCHENITSA (BULGARIA)

Dance Meaning: Wedding Ruchenitsa from Kotlen
Pronunciation: Kot-LEN-ska Svat-BAR-ska Roochen-I-tsa
Choreography: By Jim Gold using traditional steps from Bulgaria
Music: Horo Records
Formation: Line: arms in V position.
Meter: 7/8: quick/quick/slow: q,q,s
Jim Gold YouTube video: https://www.youtube.com/watch?v=Zrtn10f8CUE
Introduction: 8 measures
Measures:

FIRST STEP

1	Moving bkwd in LOD, to the right, CCW
	Hop on L(q), step back on R(q)
	step on L next to R(s)
2	Repeat meas 1
3	Moving forwards LOD, to the right, CCW
	Leap fwd on R(q), step L next to R(q)
	step fwd on R(s)
4	Repeat meas. 3
5	Facing ctr
	Hop on L, lift R(q ,q)
	hop on L, lift R, turn to face left(s)
6	step on R next to L(q), step on L next to R(q)
	step on R in place next to L(s)
7	Repeat meas. 5 using opp ft
8	Repeat meas.6 using opp ft

SECOND STEP

Moving into ctr

1	Touch R toe 2x while bouncing on L ft(q, q)
	step R next to L(s)
2	Repeat meas. 1 using opp ft,
3	step fwd on R(q, q), hop on R, lift L(s)
4	step fwd on L(q,), hop on L, lift R(s)

THIRD STEP

3 pas de pas

1	Face ctr: step R in place(q), cross L over R(q)

	step R in place(s)
2	Repeat meas. 1 opp ft
3	Repeat meas. 1
4	Jump on both ft with feet apart(q, q), lift R leg(s)
	Going bkwd out of circle: 4 pas de bas
5	step R in place(q), cross L over R(q)
	step R in place(s)
6	Repeat meas. 5 using opp ft
7-8	Repeat meas. 5-6
9-12	Circular window washing movements

Repeat meas 5-8 in place. Arms move to W position, hands perform circular window washing movement.

KURDISH BEAUTY (Kurdistan/Israel)

Choreography: Jim Gold in traditional Kurdish style
Music: Dor HaHamshik (Generations Continue). Produced by the Kurdish
    Community of Jerusalem.
Style: Heavy, bouncy
Formation: Tight line, fingers interlocked,
Meter: 2/4
Jim Gold YouTube video: *https://www.youtube.com/watch?v=o8Q0fHUeXJc*
Introduction: 7 measures
Measures:

FIRST STEP (11 counts)
    Face rt. Bouncy walk CCW, lft hand in small of back behind rt

1   Step on R (ct 1), step on L (ct 2)
2   step on R (ct 1), step on L (ct 2)
3   Step on R (ct 1), Turn, face ctr, step on L, arms down (ct 2)
4   Stamp on R (ct 1), stamp on R (ct 2)
5   Rock back on R (ct 1), rock fwd on L (ct 2)
6   Rock back on R(ct 1), rock fwd on L, and lift hands (forearms) to
    parallel to ground position (ct 2)

SECOND STEP
    Face ctr. Moving into ctr. 2 two-steps fwd

1   Step R fwd (ct 1), step L next to R (ct &), step R fwd (ct 2)
2   Step L fwd (ct 1), step R next to L (ct &), step L fwd (ct2)
3   Step R fwd (ct1), step L fwd (ct 2)
4   Stamp on R next to L (ct 1), step on R to side facing out (ct 2)
    Back 4 steps: RLRL
5   Step R back (ct 1), step L back (ct 2)
6   Repeat meas 5

THIRD STEP
    Rocking step
1   Rock fwd on R (ct 1), rock back on L (ct 2)
2-8   Repeat meas 1 7x

ORDER OF STEPS:
1. First Step 4x, Second Step: 2x, Third Step: 1x

LA KREASYON (Bosnia)

Dance Meaning: The Creation
Pronunciation: La Cray A See yon
Choreography: by Jim Gold in Bosnian/Balkan folk dance style
Music: Flory Jagoda: Arvoliko
Formation: Line, holding hands in W position
Meter: 4/4
Jim Gold YouTube video: *https://www.youtube.com/watch?v=ypPZ0XtO6dA*
Introduction: 1 measures
Measures:

FIRST STEP

1   Fall fwd on L leaning fwd (ct 1), tap rt full ft next to L (ct 2)
       Step R to rt (ct 3), step L behind R (ct 4)
2   Step R to rt (ct 1-2), tch L heel next to R leaning back (ct 3-4)
3-14   Repeat meas 1-2 6x
       Transition step
15   Fall fwd on L leaning fwd (ct 1), tap rt heel next to L (ct 2)
       Step R to rt (ct 3), step L behind R (ct 4)
16   Step R to rt (ct 1-2), lean to R (ct 3-4)
       5 Rocks and close
17   Rock left (ct 1-2), rock right (ct 3-4)
18   Rock left (ct 1-2), rock right (ct 3-4)
19   Rock left (ct 1-2), close R to L (ct 3-4)

SECOND STEP

       7's moving CW
1   Cross R over L (ct 1), step on L behind R (ct 2)
       Cross R over L (ct 3), step on L behind R (ct 4)
2   Cross R over L (ct 1), step on L behind R (ct 2)
       Cross R over L (ct 3), lift L (ct 4)
       7 moving CCW
3-4   Repeat meas 1-2 opp ft, opp dir
       7's moving into ctr
5-6   Facing ctr. Repeat meas 1-2 pattern into ctr start wi R (ct 1)
       Place left behind R heel (ct 2)
       7's out of ctr
7-8   Facing ctr. Repeat meas 5-6 pattern out of ctr but stepping
       back on L (ct 1)

— 106 —

Bring R ft next to L toe (ct 2)

8-step grapevine CCW

17   Step R to rt (ct 1), L behind rt (ct 2), step R to rt (ct 3), L in front of rt (ct 4)

18   Step R to rt (ct 1), L behind rt (ct 2) step R to rt (ct 3), L in front of rt (ct 4)

19   Step R to rt (ct 1-2), close L to rt (ct 3-4)

20   Step L to lft (ct 1-2), close R to L (ct 3-4)

Ending

1-14 **Repeat meas 1-14 of FIRST STEP**

15   Fall fwd on L leaning fwd (ct 1), tap rt heel next to L (ct 2) Step R to rt (ct 3), step L behind R (ct 4)

16   Step R to rt (ct 1-2), lean to R (ct 3-4)

3 Rocks and close

17   Rock left (ct 1-2), rock right (ct3-4)

18   Rock lft (ct 1-2), step on right (ct 3), close L to R (ct 4)

1-12 **Repeat meas 1-6 of SECOND STEP**

13   Rock to L (ct 1-2), rock to R (ct 3-4)

14   Rock L (ct 1-2), step fwd on R (ct 3), bring L next to R (ct 4)

15   Step fwd on R and hold (ct 1-4). Say "Greet your friends"

ORDER OF STEPS

1. First Step: 1x, Second Step: 1x
2. First Step: 1x, Second Step: 1x
3. First Step: 1x, Second step (as shown above)

LA PARIDA (BOSNIA)

Dance Meaning: The new mother. "La parida is the woman who is in labor. The song is about the family who is celebrating the joy of a new life and the husband who is trying to calm his wife as she is in the throes of labor and moaning that she is dying. I remember the experience well!" (Betty Murphy, daughter of Flory Jagoda).

Pronunciation: As written

Choreography: by Jim Gold in Bosnian "Ladino" folk dance style

Music: Flory Jagoda

Formation: Open circle, hands down in V position

Meter: 4/4

Jim Gold YouTube video: *https://www.youtube.com/watch?v=vVvH3m1PmGs*

Introduction: 2 measures

Measures:

FIRST STEP

"Double dip walk"

Moving in LOD, CCW: 2 walking steps, double dip step

1   Step fwd on R (ct 1), step fwd on L (ct 2)
     Step fwd on R with slight dip (ct 3)
     Step fwd on L (ct 4), step R next to L with slight dip (ct &)

2   Repeat meas 1 wi opp ft

Continue 4 walking steps

3   Step fwd on R (ct 1), L (ct 2), R (ct 3), L (ct 4)

4   Step fwd on R (ct 1), step L behind R (ct 2)

Full 2 step CW turn rt: R (ct 3), L (ct 4)

Face front: 8-crossings steps crossing: Cherkesia

5   Step R to rt (ct 1), cross L in front of R (ct 2)
     Step on R in place (ct 3), step on L next to R (ct 4)

6   Cross R over L (ct 1), step on L in place (ct 2)
     Step on r next to L (ct 3), cross L over R (ct 4)

7-12   Repeat meas 1-6

Two Bosnian rida cross steps: Facing ctr

13   Step to rt (ct 1), cross L over R (ct 2)
     Step on R to rt (ct 3), cross L over R (ct 4)

SECOND STEP

12-crossings steps crossing: Cherkesia

1   Step R to rt (ct 1), step L in front of R (ct 2)

Step on R in place (ct 3), step on L next to R (ct 4)

2   Cross R over L (ct 1), step on L in place (ct 2)
Step on r next to L (ct 3), cross L over R (ct 4)

3   step R to rt (ct 1), step L in front of R (ct 2)
Step on R in place (ct 3), step on L next to R (ct 4)
2 Stamps

4   Step on R (ct 1), stamp L next to R (ct 2)
Step on L (ct 3), stamp R next to L (ct 4)
Slow crossing: 8 crossing steps

5-7   Repeat meas 1-3
Slow 8-crossings steps crossing: Cherkesia

8   Step R to rt (ct 1), step L in front of R (ct 2),
Step on R in place (ct 3), step on L next to R (ct 4)

9   Cross R over L (ct 1), step on L in place (ct 2)
Step on R next to L (ct 3), cross L over R (ct 4)

ENDING

1-6   Repeat meas 1-6 of FIRST STEP
7   2 Bosnian rida cross steps
8 crossing steps
8   4 crossing steps
9   4 crossing steps
10   Full 4-step turn rt: CW
11   Step on R, bring L behind R calve and hold 4 cts

ORDER OF STEPS

1. First Step: 1x, Second Step: 1x
2. First Step: 1x, Second Step: 1x
3. First Step: ENDING Step

LA TORE (BOSNIA)

Dance Meaning: The Tower
Pronunciation: La Toreh
Choreography: by Jim Gold in Bosnian (Balkan) folk dance style
Music: Flory Jagoda: Kantikas Di Mi Nona
Formation: Open Circle, Hands in W position
Meter: 4/4
Jim Gold YouTube video: *https://www.youtube.com/watch?v=KkrhCmxGiCs*
Introduction: 8 meas
Measures:

FIRST STEP
    Face ctr

1   Step R to rt (ct 1), stamp lightly L next to R (ct &)
    Step L to lft (ct 2), stamp lightly R next to L (ct &)
    Step R to rt (ct 3), tap on L next to R (ct &)
    Fall fwd on L, bring R instep (ft) behind L calve (ct 4)

2   Repeat meas 1

3   Step back on R (ct 1)
    3 rocks: Rock fwd on L (ct 2), rock back on R (ct &)
    Rock fwd on L (ct 3), lift R (ct 4)
    Grapevine 5 to left, touch

4   Dip and cross R in front of L (ct 1), step L to lft side (ct &)
    Step R behind L (ct 2), step L to left side (ct &)
    Cross R in front of L with slight "hazak" dip (ct 3)
    Tch L toe behind R (ct 4)

5   **2 heels**
    Lightly tap L heel fwd (ct 1), tap L heel fwd (ct 2)
    Bring arms down to V position. Back Yemenite left
    Step back on L, arms go down to V position (ct 3),
    Step R next to L, arm stay down (ct &), step fwd on L, arms up
    to W position (ct 4)
    Grapevine 5 to left, touch, bring arms up to W position

6   Dip and cross R in front of L (ct 1), step L to lft side (ct &),
    Step R behind L (ct 2), step L to lft side (ct &),
    Cross R in front of L (ct 3), tch L behind R (ct 4)

SECOND STEP
    Touches and arms

1   Reach-tch L to lft side, glance (remez-"hint") at L ft (ct 1)

      Tch L to ctr, glance down at L (ct 2)

      Bring arms down to V position:

      Back Yemenite step

      Step back on L, arms go down to V position (ct 3),

      Step R next to L, arms stay down (ct &),

      Step fwd on L, arms up to W position (ct 4)

2   Reach-tch R to rt side (ct 1)

      Tch R to ctr, glance down at L (ct 2)

      Right Yemenite step

      Step back on R, arms down to V position (ct 3)

      Step L next to R, arms stay down (ct &)

      Step fwd on R, arms up to W position (ct 4)

      Rock and lift step

3   Step fwd on L (ct 1)

      3 rocks: Rock back on R (ct 2), rock fwd on L (ct &), step on R (ct 3), lift L (t 4)

      Grapevine 5 to right, touch

4   Dip and cross L in front of R (ct 1), step R to rt side (ct &)

      Step L behind R (ct 2), step R to rt side (ct &)

      Cross L in front of R (ct 3)

      Tch R toe far behind L as you look over lft shldr at R toe (ct 4)

ORDER OF STEPS

1. First Step: 1x, Second Step: 1x.

LAYLA, LAYLA (ISRAEL)

Dance Meaning: Night, Night,
Pronunciation: LAee-la
Choreography: by Jim Gold
Music: Layla, "Layla," performed by harmonica virtuoso Avram Barzelay accompanied on guitar by his son, Ifar Barzelay.
Formation: Circle, arms in V position
Meter: 3/4
Jim Gold YouTube video: *https://www.youtube.com/watch?v=TClBlLaVxrs*
Introduction: 4 measures
Measures:

FIRST STEP
Walking waltz step, CCW in LOD

1   Step fwd on R (ct 1), bring L next to R (ct 2), step fwd on R (ct 3)
2   Repeat meas 1 opp ft
3-4 Repeat meas 1-2
5-6 Repeat meas 1-2
     3-step full turn right, CW
7   R (ct 1), L (ct 2), R (ct 3)
     face ctr, 3-step cherkessia
8   cross L in front of R (ct 1), step on R in place (ct 2), step on L next to R (ct 3)

SECOND STEP
Into ctr, step, lift, and sway

1   Step fwd on R (ct 1), lift L (ct 2), step fwd on L (ct 3)
2   Repeat meas 1
3   **6-step cherkessia**
     Step on R (ct 1), cross L over R (ct 2), step on R in place (ct 3)
4   step on L in place (ct 1), cross R over L (ct 2), step on L in place (ct 3)
     Move bkwds out of circle
5   Step back on R (ct 1), bring L next to R (ct 2), step back on R (ct 3)
6   Repeat meas 5 opp ft
7   **3-step cherkessia**
     Step on R (ct 1), cross L over R (ct 2), step on R in place (ct 3)
8   Step on L (ct 1), slowly lift and hold R (ct 2-3)

8-step grapevine left, CW

9   Step R in front of L(ct 1), step L to left side of R (ct 2),
     step on R behind L (ct 3)
10   Step L to left (ct 1), R front of L (ct 2), L to left side of R (ct 3)
11   Step R behind L(ct 1), step L to left (ct 2), cross R over L (ct 3)
12   Step L in place (ct 1), step R in place next to L(ct 2), close L
     to R (ct 3)

THIRD STEP

1-4 Repeat meas 1-4 from Second Step
5   Moving out of circle, R shoulder facing out, step out of circle
     on R (ct 1)
     cross L in front of R (ct 2), step out of circle on R (ct 3)
6   Cross L in front of R (ct 1), step out of circle on R (ct 2), cross L in
     front of R (ct 3)
     3-step full turn right, CW
7   R (ct 1), L (ct 2), R (ct 3)
     3-step Cherkessia
8   Cross L over R (ct 1), step on R in place (ct 2), step on L in place (ct
3)

BREAK

1   Face ctr, step to R (ct 1), bring L next to R (ct 2-3)
1-28 Repeat entire dance from beginning

LULE (ALBANIA)

Dance Meaning: Flower. From song "Hodha Nje Lule Në Ferrë"—have thrown a flower to the bushes.

Pronunciation: Hodha nyë loole në ferrë ("ë" pronounced like *schwa* or "e" in "the"), "Hodha, hedh, hidhem'—have thrown, throw, I jump down! Një lule—a flower! Në ferrë—into the bush!

Choreography: by Jim Gold in Albanian folk style

Music: Irini Qirjako: Hodha nje lulë në Ferrë

Formation: Open circle, arms up, W position, Style: subtle bouncy

Meter: 4/4

Jim Gold YouTube video: *https://www.youtube.com/watch?v=t6VsOYXNVAM*

Introduction: 8 meas

Measures:

FIRST STEP

Seven Pogonishte steps, and lift

Facing fwd: seven pogonishte steps

(If done alone, solo: Arms straight, in T formation, like shoulder hold)

1	Step R to rt (ct 1-2), step L behind R (ct 3), step R to rt (ct 4)
2	Cross L over R (ct 1-2), step R next to L (ct 3), L to lft (ct 4)
3-6	Repeat meas 1-2 2x
7	Step R to rt (ct 1-2), step L behind R (ct 3), step R to rt (ct 4)
8	Step fwd on L (ct 1-2), lift R and hold (ct 3.4)

SECOND STEP

Touches, Albanite right, Albanite left

(If done alone, solo, arms down to V positions)

1	Tch R fwd (ct 1-2), tch R diag rt (ct 3-4)
2	Step back on R (ct 1), step L next to R (ct 2)
	tep fwd on R next to L (ct 3-4)
3	Tch L fwd (ct 1-2), tch L diag lft (ct 3-4)
4	Step back on L (ct 1), step R next to L (ct 2)
	step fwd on L next to R (ct 3), push-point R to diag rt (ct 4)

THIRD STEP

Move CW, facing front

1	Cross R over L (ct 1-2), step L to lft (ct 3), cross R over L (ct 4)
2	Step L to lft (ct 1-2), cross R in front of L (ct 3-4)

3	Repeat meas 2
	Albanite left (Yemenite left)
4	Step on L (ct 1), step R next to L (ct 2), cross L over R (ct 3-4)

ORDER OF STEPS

1. First Step: 1x, Second Step: 1x, Third Step: 1x
   Repeat Order of Steps 6 or 7 times

MADRE MIJA SI MI MUERO (BOSNIA)

Dance Meaning: Mother (Mine), If I Die
Pronunciation: Madre miya si me moro: Sung in Ladino.
Choreography: by Jim Gold in Bosnian (Balkan) folk dance style
Music: Flory Jagoda: Memories of Sarajevo
Formation: Open circle, Hands in W or V positions.
Meter: 2/4
Jim Gold YouTube video: *https://www.youtube.com/watch?v=TrIKCXXMNzM*
Teaneck Senior Show: *https://www.youtube.com/watch?v=b9mxf7s1RfY*
Introduction: 3 measures
Measures:

FIRST STEP

Hands in W position. (Step starts on **"muero"**)
"Rocking two-step"equals one measure, "Rock back": equals half measure, or one beat. Easy way to explain: Dance "Rocking two-step and back" 4 x
Facing and moving CCW
Rocking two-step and Rock back. Hands in V position.

1	Step to rt on R (ct 1), step L next to R (ct &), rock fwd on R (ct 2)
2	Rock back on L (ct 1), step to rt on R (ct 2), bring L next to R (ct &)
3	Rock fwd on R (ct 1), rock back on L (ct 2)
4	Step to rt on R (ct 1), step L next to R (ct &), rock fwd on R (ct 2)
5	Rock back on L (ct 1), step to rt on R (ct 2), bring L next to R (ct &)
6	Rock fwd on R (ct 1), rock back on L (ct 2)
7	Step to rt on R (ct 1), step L next to R (ct &), rock fwd on R (ct 2)
	Hands go down, arms in V position
8	Step back in L (ct 1), back on R (ct &)
	Moving CCW: 1 crossing step
	Cross L over R (ct 2), step on R next to L (ct &)
	2 crossing steps and lift
9	Cross L over R (ct 1), step on R next to L(ct &)
	Cross L over R (ct 2), lift R (ct &)
10	Cross R over L (ct 1), step on L next to R (ct &)
	Cross R over L (ct 2), step on L next to R (ct &)

SECOND STEP

Grapevine
1	Cross R over L (ct 1), step on L next to R (ct &)

Step on R behind L (ct 2), step on L next to R (ct &)
Crossing step

2   Cross R over L (ct 1), step on L next to R (ct &)

        Cross R over L (ct 2), step on L next to R (ct &)

3   Repeat meas 1

4   Cross R over L (ct 1), step on L next to R (ct &)

        Cross R over L (ct 2), lift L (ct &)

        Grapevine CCW

5   Cross L over R (ct 1), step on R next to L (ct &)

        Step on L behind R (ct 2), step on R next to L (ct &)

6   **Crossing step**

        Cross L over R (ct 1), step on R next to L (ct &)

        Cross L over R (ct 2), place R instep next to L calve (ct &)

THIRD STEP

        Three 2-steps, and hold

        Hands in W position. Moving CCW

1   Step on R (ct 1), bring L next to R (ct &)

        Step on R (ct 2), place L instep on R calve (ct &)

2   Step on L (ct 1), bring R next to L (ct &)

        Step on L(ct 2), place R instep on L calve (ct &)

3   Step on R (ct 1), bring L next to R (ct &)

        Step on R (ct 2), place L instep on R calve (ct &)

4   Step fwd on L, hold R ft behind L calve (ct 1-2)

ORDER OF STEPS:

1. First Step: 1x, Second Step: 1x, Third Step: 1x
2. First Step: 1x, Second Step: 1x, Third Step: 1x
3. First Step: 1x, Second Step: 1x,

        ENDING

6   **Crossing step**

        Cross L over R (ct 1), step on R next to L (ct &)

        Cross L over R (ct 2)

7   Step into ctr on R to rt(ct 1), step on L behind R (ct &)

        Step on R to rt, tch L behind R calve, and hold (2)

MAI NEICUTA MAI GORJENE (ROMANIA)

Dance Meaning: My Dear Gorjene, or, My Sweetheart from Gorj
Pronunciation: Maee Neykuta Maee Goryene
Choreography: by Jim Gold in Romania folk dance style
Music: Cimbalom Traditions: Alexander Fedoriouk
Formation: Line. High hands: (W position)
Meter: 4/4
Jim Gold YouTube video: https://www.youtube.com/watch?v=efSsFMNsMYM
Introduction: 8 measures
Measures:

FIRST STEP

Hora and Grapevine: Move diag to Rt

1   Hora: Walk diag rt and fwd: R(ct 1), L(ct 2), R(ct 3), tch L
        next to R(ct 4)

2   Walk diag rt and backward: L(ct 1), R(ct 2), L(ct 3), tch R to L(ct 4)

3-4   Repeat meas 1-2

        Grapevine 8

5   Step R to R(ct 1), step L behind R(ct 2), step R to rt(ct 3), step L
        in front of R(ct 4)

6   Repeat meas 5

7-8   Repeat meas 1-2

SECOND STEP

1   Face ctr: Step R to rt(ct 1), step L behind R(ct 2), step R ro rt(ct 3),
        lift L (optional flutter kick)(ct 4)

2   Repeat Step 1 opp dir

3-4   Repeat meas 1-2

5   Step on R to rt(ct 1), stamp L next to R(ct 2), step L to lft(ct 3),
        stamp R next to L(ct 4)

6   Repeat meas 5

7   Repeat meas 1

8   Step L to left(ct 1), step R behind L(ct 2),
        Step on L in place(ct 3), stamp on R next to L(ct 4)

ORDER OF STEPS:
1. First Step: 1x, Second Step: 1x

MAICA (ROMANIA)

Dance Meaning: Mother
Pronunciation: MAI-ka
Music: Bijuterii Folclorice: Muntenia si Oltenia
Choreography: By Jim Gold using traditional steps from Romania.
Formation: Open circle holding hands in W position
Meter: 4/4
Jim Gold YouTube video: *https://www.youtube.com/watch?v=rlR9KGrQOpE*
Palisades Folk Dancers Jim Gold's Maica:
https://www.youtube.com/watch?v=SsQBuxRN1cs
Introduction: 8 measures
Measures:

FIRST STEP

Moving diag right into circle
2 two-steps
1   Step forward on R (ct 1), bring L next to R (ct &), step forward
     on R (ct 2) step forward on L (ct 3), bring R next to L (ct &), step
     forward on R (ct 4)
2 lift steps
2   R (ct 1) , lift L (ct 2), step L (ct 3), lift R (ct 4)
Moving diag right out of circle
3   R (ct 1), L (ct 2), R (ct 3), L (ct 4)
4-6 Repeat meas 1-3

SECOND STEP

Into ctr
1   R (ct 1), lift L (ct 2), R (ct 3), lift L (ct 4)
Moving left, CW
2   Cross R over L (ct 1), step on L (ct 2), cross R over L (ct 3), step
     on L (ct 4)
Moving out of circle
3   Cross R over L (ct 1), step on L (ct 2), cross R over L (ct 3),
     step on L (ct 4)
Continue out of circle with a 3-step grapevine
4   Cross R over L (ct 1), step on L next to R (ct 2)
     Face ctr. step on R next to L (ct 3), step on L in place (ct 4)
5-8 Repeat meas 1-4

THIRD STEP

        Two grapevines, moving to left, CW

1   Step on R over L (ct 1), step on L next to R (ct 2)

        step on R behind L (ct 3), step on L next to R (ct 4)

2   Repeat meas 1

        Continue left with 2 two-steps, CW

3   R (ct 1), L (ct &), R (ct 2), L (ct 3), R (ct &), L (ct 4)

        One grapevine, moving to left, CW

4   Cross R over L (ct 1), step on L next to R (ct 2),

        Step on R behind L(ct 3), step on L next to R(ct 4)

Presented by Jim Gold at the Florida Folk Dance Camp, February 2004.

MAN OF CONSTANT SORROW (USA)

Choreography: Jim Gold in USA Country and Western style
Music: Man of Constant Sorrow sung by Ralph Stanley
Formation: Line dance, no hand hold
Meter: 2/4
Jim Gold YouTube video: *https://www.youtube.com/watch?v=nXQkyHSKyWM*
Introduction: 5 meas
Measures:

FIRST STEP

Facing ctr: 2 Sides (csardas)

1   Step R to rt (ct 1), close L to R (ct &),
     Step R to rt (ct 2), tap L next to R (ct &)

2   Step L to lft (ct 1), close R to L (ct &)
     Step L to lft (ct 2), tap R next to L (ct &)

3-4 Repeat meas 1-2

3 Yemenite moving fwd (3x)

5   Step R to rt (ct 1), close L to R (ct &)
     Cross R over L moving fwd (ct 2)

6   Step l to lft (ct 1), close R to L (ct &)
     Cross L over R moving fwd (ct 2)

7   Step R to rt (ct 1), close L to R (ct &)
     Cross R over L moving fwd (ct 2)

Slap step, and back

8   Tch L to lft, L hand fwd (ct 1), lift L, slap R hand to L boot (ct 2)

Walk back

9   Step back L (ct 1), R (ct 2)

10   Step L (ct 1), R (ct &), L (ct 2), tch R next to L (ct &)

11-20 Repeat meas 1-10

11a   Extra measure: Pause step: Step R to rt (ct 1), close L to R (ct 2)

11-20 Repeat meas 1-10

SECOND STEP

4 two-steps fwd. In "slight diagonals"
Moving into ctr

1   Step R fwd (ct 1) bring L next to R (ct &)
     Step R fwd (ct 2)

2   Step L fwd (ct 1) bring R next to L (ct &), step L fwd (ct 2)

3-4 Repeat meas 1-2

Cherkassia 8

5   Cross R front of L (ct 1), step L in place (ct &)

        Step R side of L(ct 2), step L in place(ct &)

6   Repeat meas 5

        Sides and slaps

        Moving to rt. CCW

7   Step to R (ct 1), L behind R (ct &)

        Step R to rt(ct 2) stamp L(ct &)

        Moving to lft. CW

8   Step to L(ct 1), R behind L(ct &)

        Step L to lft (ct 2) slap inside of R boot with outside of lft hand (ct &)

        Walk back and 4 off-beat slaps

9   Step back on R (ct 1), slap R hand across L thigh (ct &)

        Step back on L (ct 2), slap R hand cross R thigh (ct &)

10   Step back on R (ct 1), slap R hand across L thigh (ct &)

        Step back on L (ct 2), slap R hand cross R thigh (ct &)

11a   **Extra measure: Pause step:** Step R to rt (ct 1), close L to R (ct 2)

11-20 Repeat meas 1-10 of Part II

ORDER OF STEPS

1. First Step: 2x, Second Step

MILA MAMO NUMBER ONE (Macedonia)

Dance Name: Ne Moi Ma, Mila Mamo, Lyooto Da Kolnesh
Dance Meaning: Dear mother, don't curse me bitterly. Title translation by Martha
   Forsyth. ma = dialect form of "mene" (me), lyooto = fiercely (adverb),
   kolnesh (k'lnesh) = curse (verb) Nemoi, as far as I know, is a single word. It
   introduces a negative imperative ("DON'T [do x]")
Pronunciation: Ne Moy Ma, Meela Mamo
Choreography: by Jim Gold in Macedonian folk dance style
Music: Makedonski Pesni with Stoyan Djadjev and "Shtchooro Make."
Formation: Open circle, hands in W position
Meter: 2/4
Jim Gold YouTube video: *https://www.youtube.com/watch?v=fyiihaJn1i4*
Introduction: 4 measures
Measures:

FIRST STEP
Moving diag in and out of ctr

1   R (ct 1), L (ct &), R(ct 2), lift L(ct &)
2   L (ct 1), R (ct &), L (ct 2), lift R (ct &)

4 steps out of ctr

3   Diag out of ctr: R (ct 1), L (ct &), R (ct 2), L (ct &)
4   R (ct 1), lift L (ct &), step on R (ct 2), lift L (ct &)
5-7   Repeat meas 1-3
8   R (ct 1), L (ct &), tch R to left instep (ct 2)

SECOND STEP
Moving CCW
Balance (sway) grapevine and lifts

1   Balance (sway) to rt on R (ct 1), balance (sway) lft on L (ct 2)

7 step grapevine CCW

2   R to rt (ct 1), L front of R (ct &), step R (ct 2), L behind R (ct 2)
3   R to rt (ct 1), L front of R (ct &), step R balance (sway) (ct 2)
4   Step L to left (ct 1), R behind L (ct &), step L (ct 2)
   Point R to rt (ct &)
5   **Cherkasia 4**
   Cross R front of L (ct 1), step L in place (ct &)
   Step R next to L (ct 2), step L across R (ct &)

ORDER OF STEPS
1. First Step: 2x, Second Step: 4x

MI SE SOBRALE (MACEDONIA)

Dance Meaning: (We gather)
Choreography: by Jim Gold in Macedonian folk dance style
Formation: Line: arms in V and W position
Meter: 9/8 quick/slow/quick/quick: q, s, q, q (or q, qq, q, q, q)
Jim Gold YouTube video: *https://www.youtube.com/watch?v=OfhU74UvYcQ*
Introduction: 8 measures. Begin with Second Step, or start right away with meas 1.
Measures:

FIRST STEP

Moving to the right, CCW: Arms down in V position

1   Step on R (q), step on L (q q), hop on L (q)
      Run fwd on R (q), run fwd on L (q)

2-3 Repeat meas 1 2x

4   Face ctr, step on R (q), snap-close L to R (s)
      2 push steps to the left, CW with weight still on R
      fall on L and close R to L (q), fall on L (q)

5-9 Repeat meas 1-4

SECOND STEP

Facing ctr: Floating step, arms up in W position

1   Step fwd on R (q), lift L in front of R (s)
      Lift on R while bringing L back in a reel step (q), step on L
      behind R (q)

2   Lift R in front of L (q)
      Bring R back in a reel step (s)
      Step on R behind L (q)
      Step on L next to R (q)

3-4 Repeat meas 1-2

THIRD STEP

8 crossing steps, cherkessia

1   Facing ctr: cross R over L (q), step on L in place (s)
      Step on R next to L (q), cross L over R (q)

2   Step on L in place (q), step R next to L (s)
      Cross R over L (q), step on L in place (q)

3-4 Repeat meas 1-2

FOURTH STEP

1-8 Repeat Second Step 2x

MOLDAVIAN HORA LUI AURESCU (ROMANIA)

Dance Meaning: Circle Dance from Moldavia
Pronunciation: Moldavian Hora Lou-i Ow-resk-yew
Choreography: by Jim Gold in Romanian folk dance style
Music: Source unknown
Formation: Open Circle, arms in W position
Meter: 4/4
Jim Gold YouTube video: *https://www.youtube.com/watch?v=3L9yvr3mNlI*
Introduction: 4 measures
Measures:

FIRST STEP
Walk into ctr 4 steps. Shaking (twisting) head rt and left
1   Step on R in place (ct 1), L (ct 2), R (ct 3), L (ct 4)
2   Step on R (ct 1), lift L (ct 2), step on L (ct 3), lift R (ct 4)
Walk bkwds 4 steps
3   Step back on R (ct 1), L (ct 2), R (ct 3), L (ct 4)
4   Step on R in place (ct 1), lift L (ct 2), Step on L in place (ct 3)
twist-stamp step: stamp on R next to L twisting rt leg diag left (ct &)
Step on R twisting diag to rt no weight (ct 4)
5-8   Repeat meas 1-4

SECOND STEP
Grapevine and two-step. Moving left
1   **Grapevine:** Step R over L (ct 1),step L to left side (ct 2)
Step R behind L (ct 3), step L to left side (ct 4)
2 two steps. Continuing left
2   Step on R (ct 1), step on L (ct &), step on R (ct 2)
Step on L (ct 3), step on R (ct &), step on L (ct 4)
3   Repeat meas 1
4   **1 two-step:** Step on R (ct 1), step on L (ct &), step on R (ct 2)
Face ctr: step on L (ct 3), bring R next to L (ct 4)
5-8   Repeat meas 1-4 opp dir, opp ft

THIRD STEP
Facing ctr, syncopated clap and slap step
1   Step R to rt (ct 1), clap (ct &)
Bring L next to R (ct 2), clap (ct &)
Step R to rt (ct 3), clap (ct &)

	Clap again. bring L next to R (ct 4)
2	Repeat meas 1 opp. dir, opp. ft
3-4	Repeat meas 1-2
5	Repeat meas 1-4
	Hold R hand above head (prepare to slap left inner calf)
	Step R to rt (ct 1), slap outer L thigh with left hand (ct &)
	Bring L next to R (ct 2), slap outer L thigh with left hand (ct &)
	Step to R to rt (ct 3)
	Slap outer left thigh again with L hand (ct &)
	Slap inner left calf with R hand (ct 4)
	Slap outer left thigh with L hand (ct &)
6	Repeat meas 5 opp dir, opp ft with same hand slaps
7-8	Repeat meas 5-6

ORDER OF STEPS

1. First Step: 1x, Second Step: 1x, Third Step: 1x
2. First Step: 1x, Second Step: 1x, Third Step: 1
3. First Step: 1x, Second Step: 1x, Third Step: 1x
4. First Step: 1x (Ending)

MULTSU MESC (ROMANIA)

Dance Meaning: Thank You
Pronunciation: Multsumesk
Choreography: by Jim Gold in Moldavian Bruil folk dance style
Music: Unknown
Formation: Line
Meter: 2/4
Jim Gold YouTube video: *http://bit.ly/2mTScC8*
Introduction: Talking. Then 8 measure music intro
Measure:

SLOW PART
FIRST STEP
Striding: Broad walking steps. swing arms from shoulders,
elbows straight, move CCW in circle.

1   Step R (ct 1), Step L (ct 2)
2-8   Repeat meas 1 7x

SECOND STEP
Move CCW in the circle: Two back pas de bas and walks

1   Step R (ct 1), step L behind R (ct &), step R (ct 2), arms move to rt in windshield wiper movement
2   Repeat meas 1, but arms move left
3-4   **Walk 4 steps, arms swing:** R (ct 1), L (ct 2), R (ct 1), L (ct 2)
5-16   Repeat meas 1-4 3x

THIRD STEP
"Knead the dough": Walk CCW in circle with "Knead dough" movement

1   Step R (ct 1), left arm straight fwd palm up, rt arm straight fwd palm down.
Step L (ct 2), reverse arms (left arm straight fwd palm down, rt arm straight fwd palm up.
2-4   Repeat meas 1 3x
5-8   Repeat meas 1-2
9-12   Repeat meas 1-2 2x of SECOND STEP
13-16   Repeat meas 1-4

FAST PART
FIRST STEP

Romanian basic hora: Moving like a V diag fwd and diag back
Hands in V position.

1   Step R diag fwd (ct 1), step L (ct 2)
2   Step R (ct 1), tch L next to R (ct 2)
3   Step L diag back (ct 1), step R (ct 2)
    Step L (ct 1), tch R next to L (ct 2)

SECOND STEP

Sides and 8-step grapevine: (Solo dancing: Arms in T formation)

1   Face ctr. Step R to rt (ct 1), L behind R (ct 2)
2   R to rt (ct 1), stamp L (ct 2)
3   Step L to lft (ct 1), R behind L (ct 2)
4   L to lft (ct 1), lift R (ct 2)
5-6 R over L (ct 1), L to side (ct 2), R behind L (ct 1), L to side (ct 2)
7-8 R over L (ct 1), L to side (ct 2), R behind L (ct 1), L to side (ct 2)
9-16 Repeat meas 1-8

THIRD STEP

Calusari step: (Solo dancing: Hands on hips)

1   Hop on R, lift L (ct 1), step R (ct &), step on 2 (ct 2)
2   Repeat meas 1
3   Cross R over L (ct 1), step on L in place (ct 2)
4   Step R next to L (ct 1), step on L in place (ct 2)
5-6 Repeat meas 1-2
    Hop and run in place 7 steps
7-8 Hop on L (ct 1), step on R (ct &), L (ct 2), R (ct &)
    L (ct 1), R (ct &), L (ct 2), R (ct &)
9-12 Repeat meas 1-4
13-14 Repeat meas 1-2
15-16 Repeat meas 7-8

ORDER OF STEPS

Slow First Part: Order as written above
Second Part: First Step: 4x, Second Step: 2x, Third Step: 1x
First step: 4x, Second Step 2x, Third Step 1x
Speeds up: First step: 4x, Second Step 2x, Third Step 1x

NAXOS KALIMERA (GREECE)

Dance Meaning: Good morning Naxos
Pronunciation: Naksos Kaleemera
Choreography: by Jim Gold in Greek folk dance style
Music:
Formation: Line, hands in W position
Meter: 7/8, s/q, q
Mood: restrained excitement
Style: Broad steps, defining and accented Syrtos steps.
Jim Gold YouTube video: *https://www.youtube.com/watch?v=66eICHqbVW0*
Introduction; 8 measures

FIRST STEP
Walk 3 steps CCW, and lift
1   Face CCW: Step fwd on R (s), fwd on L (q, q)
2   Fwd on R (s), lift L (q, q)
3   Step L in place (s), tch R to rt out-side (q, q)
4   Tch R fwd (s), tch R to side out-side (q, q)

SECOND STEP
Syrtos: Moving CCW
1   Face ctr: Step to R (s), step L behind R (q), step R to rt (q)
2   Face CCW: Hop on R, step on L (s), step fwd R (q), step fwd LR (q)
3   Step R in place (s), step L in front (q), step R in place (q)
4   Step back on L (s), step back on R (q), step on L in place (q).

THIRD STEP
To sides, two back pas de bas
1   Face ctr: Step R to rt (s), bring L next to R (q, q)
2   Repeat meas 1
3   Step R to rt (s), step L behind R (q), step on R in place (q)
4   Repeat meas 3 opp dir, opp ft

FOURTH STEP
Repeat SECOND STEP

ORDER OF STEPS
1. First Step: 2x, Second Step: 2x, Third Step: 2x, Fourth Step: 2x

NE KLEPEĆI (BOSNIA HERZEGOVINA)

Dance Meaning: "Ne klepeci nanulama" is bit tricky...'Don't rattle with your wooden slippers. "Nanula" is a wooden slipper worn outdoors. (Translation: Gabrijela Golub)

Pronunciation: Ne Klepetshi Nanulama

Choreography: by Jim Gold in Bosnian folk style

Music: Starogradski Biseri (Old Town Pearls) Najljepse Starogradski Pjesme CD purchased in gas station in Gabriela's home city of Banja Luka.

Formation: Open circle, arms in W position

Jim Gold YouTube video: *http://bit.ly/2n7KvH7*

Teaching: *http://bit.ly/2nfL5Sy*

Meter: 4/4

Introduction: 8 measures

Measures:

      FIRST STEP: Diagonal "V" step, move diagonally into ctr

          Step diag fwd on R (ct 1), step on L (ct 2) step fwd on R (ct 3-4)

          Step fwd on L (ct 1-2)

          Move diagonally out of the circle

3   Back on R (ct 3), back on L (ct 4)

          Step back on R (ct 1-2), step back on L (ct 3-4)

          Sway

          Sway R (ct 1-2), sway L (ct 3-4)

          2 two-steps CCW

          R (ct 1), L (ct 2), R (ct 3-4)

          L (ct 1), R (ct 2), L (ct 3-4)

          Step R (ct 1-2), L behind R (ct 3) and bring rt toe front of L (ct 4)

          Repeat First Step 3x

    SECOND STEP

1-6   Repeat meas 1-6 from step one

          4 step grapevine

7-8   Step R to rt (ct 1-2), step L behind R (ct 3-4)

          Step R to side (ct 1-2), step L in front (ct 3-4)

ORDER OF STEPS

1. First Step: 3x, Second Step: 1x

Lyrics:

Ne silazi sa cardaka i ne pitaj gdje sam bio zasto su mi oci placne zbog cega sam suzelio
Stajao sam kraj mezara i umrlu majku zvao nosio joj dar od srca ali joj ga nisam dao

Refrain:

Ne klepeci nanulama kad silazis sa cardaka sve pomislim moja draga da silazi stara majka

English translation:

Don't come down from the stabbur
And don't ask where I was
Why I've got teary eyes
Nor why I've shed tears
I stood next to her grave
And called for my mother who passed away
I brought her a gift from my heart But I didn't give it to her

Refrain

Don't rattle with your wooden slippers
When you come down from the upper porch I keep thinking, my dear
That my old mother is coming down the stairs

NENADOVA KOLO (SERBIA)

Dance Meaning: "Unexpected." Girl's name.
Pronunciation: Nena dova
Choreography: Jim Gold in Serbian U Sest style
Music: Branimir Djokic
Formation: Open circle
Meter: 4/4
Jim Gold YouTube video: *https://bit.ly/2YfYkFW*
Jim Gold YouTube teaching: *https://bit.ly/2JJK5pU*
Introduction: 8 measures
Measures:

FIRST STEP
Basic U Sest step, facing front, moving CCW:
1   Step R to rt (ct 1), step L across R (ct 2), step R to rt (ct 3), tch L
     next to R (ct 4)
2   Step L to lft (ct 1), tch R next to L (ct 2), step R to rt (ct 3), tch L
     next to R (ct 4)
3-4 Repeat meas 1-2 opp dir opp ft
5-8 Repeat meas 1-4

SECOND STEP
Serbian two-steps
1   Step R to rt (ct 1), step L across R (ct 2)   R (ct 3), L (ct &) , R (ct 4)
2   L (ct 1), R (ct &), L (ct 2), R (ct 1), L (ct &). R (ct 4)
3-4 Repeat meas 1-2, opp dir opp ft
5-8 Repeat meas 1-4

THIRD STEP
Back 8's
1   Step R to rt (ct 1), step L across R (ct 2)   R (ct 3), L (ct &) , R (ct 4)
2   8 small steps back: L (ct 1,) R (ct &), L (ct 2), R (ct &)
     L (ct 3), R (ct &), L (ct 4), R (ct &)
3   Step L to lft (ct 1), step R across L (ct 2) L (ct 3), R (ct &) , L (ct 4)
4   8 small steps back: R (ct 1,) L (ct &), R (ct 2), L (ct &),
     R (ct 3), L (ct &), R (ct 4), L (ct &)
5-8 Repeat meas 1-4

FOURTH STEP

Lifts and jiggle, and stamp

1   Step R to rt (ct 1), step L across R (ct 2), step R to rt (ct 3), lift and jiggle L (ct 4)

2   Step on L (ct 1), lift and jiggle R (ct 2), step R to rt (ct 3), lift and jiggle L (ct 4)

3-4 Repeat mea 1-2 opp dir, opp ft

5-8 Repeat meas 1-4

FIFTH STEP

Stamp, 7's fwd, 3 push steps

1   R Step R to rt (ct 1), step L across R (ct 2), step R to rt (ct 3), stamp L (ct 4)

2   **7 small steps fwd:** L (ct 1), R (ct &), L (ct 2), R (ct &), L (ct 3), R (ct &), L (ct 4)

3   Fall fwd on R (ct 1-2)

     3 push steps back

     Fall on L and push R (ct 3), step on R (ct 4)

4   Fall on L and push R (ct 1), step on R (ct 2)

     Fall on L and push R (ct 3), step on R (ct 4)

5-8 Repeat meas 1-4

SIXTH STEP

Basic U Sest 1x, touch and wiggle step 1x

1   Step R to rt (ct 1), step L across R (ct 2), step R to rt (ct 3), tch L next to R (ct 4)

2   Step L to lft (ct 1), tch R next to L (ct 2), step R to rt (ct 3), tch L next to R (ct 4)

3-4 Repeat meas 1-2 opp dir opp ft

     Touch and wiggle step 1x

5   R Step R to rt (ct 1), step L across R (ct 2), step R to rt (ct 3). ch L next to R (ct 4)

6   Fall on L, and push R turning rt ankle to rt (ct 1-2)

     Place R toe front of L and **wiggle** (ct 3-4)

7   Wiggle 4 more counts (ct 1-4)

8   **4 crosses:** Cross R over L (ct 1), step L to lft (ct 2)

     Cross R over L (ct 3), step L to lft (ct 4)

SEVENTH STEP

    Moving CCW

1	Step R to rt (ct 1), step L to lft (ct 2), step R (ct 3), L (ct &), R (ct 4)
2	Repeat step 1, continue CCW opp ft
3-4	Repeat meas 1-2)
5-8	Repeat meas 1-4

ORDER OF STEPS

1. First Step: 2x, 2. Second Step: 3. 2x, Third Step: 2x, 4. Fourth Step: 2x, 5. Fifth Step: 2x, 6. Sixth Step: 2x, 7. Seventh Step: 2x

2. First Step: 2x, 2. Second Step: 3. 2x, Third Step: 2x, 4. Fourth Step: 2x, 5. Fifth Step: 2x, 6. Sixth Step: 2x, Seventh Step 2x.

Ending: Fifth Step 2x, Sixth step 1x

O SOLE MIO (ITALY)

Dance Meaning: Oh, my Sun
Pronunciation: Oh Soleh Mee oo
Choreography: by Jim Gold in eclectic South Italian folk dance style
Music: O Sole Mio: La Tarantella. Produced 2002
Formation: Open circle. Hands in W or V position,
Style: Big sweeping steps
YouTube Video: *http://bit.ly/2olipsj*
Meter: 4/4)
Introduction: 2 measures
Measures:

FIRST STEP

Fwd and back: (Quick, quick, slow), arms in W position (T for leader)

1   Step fwd on R (ct 1), bring L next to R (ct &)
Step fwd on R (ct 2), place L ankle behind R knee (ct &)
Step back on L (3), bring R next to L (ct &)
Step back on L (ct 4), tch R toe diag to L ankle (ct &)

2   **Back pas de bas: (Slow, quick, quick)**
Step to rt on R pushing up on on R (ct 1), step L behind R (ct 2), R in place (ct &)
Step to lft on L pushing up on L (ct 3), R behind L (ct 4), L in place (ct &)

2 "rida" crosses (up-down)

3   Cross R over L pushing up on R ft (ct 1), step L behind R (ct &)
Cross R over L pushing up on R ft (ct 2), step L behind R (ct &)
4-step grapevine
Cross R over L pushing up on R (ct 3), step L to side of R (ct &)
Step on R behind L (ct 4), step L to lft (ct &)

4   **4 rocks: Arms in V position**
Rock rt (ct 1), rock lft (ct 2), rock rt (ct 3), rock lft (ct 4)

SECOND STEP

Moving LOD, CCW

1   **Facing front: Two-side step and lift, arms remain in V position**
R to rt (ct 1), step L behind R (ct &), step R to rt (ct 2), Lift L/hold (ct 3)
7-step grapevine CCW

	Cross L over R (ct 4), step R next to L (ct &)
2	Step L behind R (ct 1), step R next to L (ct &)
	Cross L over R (ct 2), step R next to L (ct &)
	Step L behind R (ct 3), lift R (ct 4)

Fwd and back

3	Step fwd on R (ct 1), bring L next to R (ct &), step fwd on R (ct 2)
	Step back on L (3), bring R next to L (ct &), step back on L (ct 4)
4	**4 rocks**
	Rock rt (ct 1), rock lft (ct 2), rock rt (ct 3), rock lft (ct 4)
5-8	Repeat meas 1-4

THIRD STEP

1-4	Repeat meas 1-4 of FIRST STEP

Fwd and spread arms/cross heart step

5	Step fwd on R (optional kneel on L knee) (ct 1-2), spread arms (ct 3-4)
6	(Stay kneeling) R hand crosses heart (ct 1-2), rise (ct 3-4)
7-8	Repeat meas 3-4 of FIRST STEP

4 rocks, arms in V position

	Rock rt (ct 1), rock lft (ct 2), rock rt (ct 3), rock lft (ct 4)
9-12	Repeat meas 1-4

Ending

After THIRD STEP (meas 1-7)

8	Rock rt (ct 1), rock lft (ct 2) ,step fwd on R (ct 3), spread arms wide (ct 4)

ORDER OF STEPS

1. First Step: 1x, Second Step: 2x, Third Step: 1x, First Step: 1x
2. Second Step: 2x, Third Step: 1x. End on one knee (optional)

OILDO MI NOVYA (BOSNIA)

Dance Meaning: I heard my girlfriend
Pronunciation: Oyldo Me Novya
Choreography: by Jim Gold in Bosnian/Greek folk dance style
Music: Sung in Ladino, language of Sephardic Jews, by Flory Jagoda
Formation: Open circle
Meter: 7/8 slow/quick/quick: s, q, q
Mood (Feeling): Calm and inward
Style: Small-stepped "soft" syrtos
Jim Gold YouTube video: *https://www.youtube.com/watch?v=u3jiMRYGZDk*
Introduction: 2 measures
Measures:

FIRST STEP

Syrtos: Moving CCW

1   Face ctr: Step to R (s), step L behind R (q), step R to rt (q)
2   Face CCW: Hop on R, step on L (s), step fwd R (q), step fwd L (q)
3   Step R in place (s), step L in front (q), step R in place (q)
4   Step back on L (s), step back on R (q), step on L in place (q)
5-8   Repeat meas 1-4

Walking

9   Step fwd on R (s), fwd on L (q), fwd on R (q)
10   Step fwd on L (s), fwd on R (q), fwd on L (q)
11   Face ctr: Step R to rt side, bring L next to R (q, q)
12   Repeat meas 11 opp ft. opp dir
13   Tch R toe in—rt heel out (s), tch R toe out—heel in (q, q)

SECOND STEP

1   Tch R toe in (s), tch R toe out (q q)

Reel back

2   Reel back on R, step on R behind L (s)
      Reel back on L (q), step R next to L (q)
3-4   Repeat meas 1-2 opp. ft.
5-8   Syrtos: Repeat meas 1-4 of FIRST STEP
9-10   Walking: Repeat meas 9-10 of FIRST STEP
11   Step to rt on R (s), bring lft tog. next to R (q, q)

ORDER OF STEPS

1. First Step: 1x, Second Step: 3x

2. First Step" 1x, Second Step: 3x
3. First Step: 1x, Second Step: 1x
16 meas ending
Dance Second step 1x (11 meas), then "1/2 x" (5 extra meas At end, step on R and
  hold.

ONIRO TIS NYCHTAS (GREECE)

Dance Meaning: Dreams of Night
Pronunciation: O-neer-oh tees, nih-tas
Choreography: Jim Gold in Greek folk dance style
Music: Constantin Paravanos: Greece (Music Around the World)
Formation: Open circle, dancers hands in W positions, V position as indicated
Meter: 9/8 (q,q,q,s)
Jim Gold YouTube link: *http://bit.ly/2pHZJE6*
Style: Heavy. sensual,
Introduction; Clap out 8 measures (q, q, q, s), then dance Third Step (2 measures)
Measures:

FIRST STEP
Into ctr and back, hands in W position

1   Into ctr: R (ct q), L (ct q), R (ct q), tch L toe fwd (ct s)
2   Back: L (ct q), R (ct q), L (ct q), tch R toe next to L
       R toe facing diag rt (ct s)

Grapevine CCW

3   Step R to rt (ct q), L behind R (ct q), R to rt side (ct q)
       L cross front of R (ct s)
4   Step R to rt (ct q), L behind R (ct q), R to rt (ct q)
       Tch L toe next to R, R toe faces front (ct s)

SECOND STEP
Into ctr and back

5   Into ctr: L (ct q), R (ct q), L (ct q), tch R toe fwd (ct s)
6   Back: R (ct q), L (ct q), R (ct q)
       Tch L toe next to R, L toe facing diag lft (ct s)

Grapevine CW, hands in V position

7   Step L to lft (ct q), R behind L (ct q), L to lft (ct q)
       R cross front of L (ct s)
8   Step L to lft (ct q), R behind L (ct q), L to lft (ct q)
       Close R to L, R ft facing ctr (ct s)

THIRD STEP
Lift step

9   Lift R(ct q, q), step R to rt(ct q), close L to R (ct s)
10   Lift R(ct q, q), step R to rt(ct q), close L to R (ct s)

ORDER OF STEPS
1. First Step: 2x, Second Step:1x, Third Step

ORAWA (POLAND)

Dance Meaning: Name of river. From Finnish word for squirrel
Pronunciation: O-ra-va
Choreography: By Jim Gold. South Poland, Zakopane folk dance style
Source: Southern Poland, Zakopane and Dunajec River region
Music: Biesiada Goralska: Orawa
Formation: Open Circle, arms in V position
Meter: 4/4
Jim Gold YouTube video: *https://www.youtube.com/watch?v=JfrKPt1Ror8*
Introduction: 8 measures
Measures:

FIRST STEP
Zakopane csardas step

1 Face ctr: Step R to the right (ct 1)
   Bring L to R (ct 2)
   Step R to the right (ct 3)
   Touch L to R (ct 4)

2 Repeat meas 1 opp ft and opp dir

3-4 Repeat meas 1-2

Dunajec river boat shuffle step

5 Step R (ct 1),tap-brush L (ct &)
   Step L (ct 2), tap/brush R (ct &)
   Step R (ct 3),tap-brush L (ct &)
   Step L (ct 4), tap-brush R (ct &)

6-8 Repeat meas 1 3x

9-10 Repeat meas 1-2

11-12 Repeat meas 1-2

SECOND STEP
Slovak sun shielding circle shuffle step

1-2 Make complete circle to right, arms up, palms flat, shade eyes from sun, repeat Dunajec river boat shuffle step footwork from First Step, measures 5-8,

3 Bent wrists on hips: shuffle step into ctr (ct 1-4)

4 Bent wrists on hips: back out of ctr
   No shuffle step (ct 1-4)

THIRD STEP

Down-the-Dunajec two-step

1   Step diag to right on R (ct 1)
     Step on L behind R (ct &)
     Step slightly fwd on R (ct 2)
     Step diag to left on L (ct 3)
     Step on R behind L (ct &)
     Step slightly fwd on L (ct 4)
2-4 Repeat meas 1 3x
     Step, Lift
5   Step fwd on R (ct 1), lift L in big sweep (ct 2)
     Step diag to left on L (ct 3)
     Bring R behind L (ct &)
     Step slightly fwd on L (ct 4)
6-8 Repeat meas 1 3x
9   Step fwd on R (ct 1), lift L in big sweep (ct 2)
     Step fwd on L (ct 3), big sweep lift R (ct 4)
10   Repeat meas 5

ORDER OF STEPS

First Step: 2x, Second Step:3x, Third Step:1x
First Step: 1x, Second Step:3x, Third Step:1x,
First Step:1x, Third Step:1x,
Ending: measures 11-12

Ending:

11   Touch R heel forward (ct 1-2)
     touch R heel to R side (ct 3-4)
12   Touch R heel forward (ct 1)
     touch R heel forward (ct 2)
     place and hold R heel to R side (ct 3-4)

OY, BABOUSHKA (RUSSIA)

Dance Meaning: Oh, Grandma!
Pronunciation: Oye, BA-booshka
Choreography: By Jim Gold using traditional steps from Russia
Music: the Mayan
Formation: Open circle
Meter: 4/4
Jim Gold YouTube video: *https://www.youtube.com/watch?v=fnwVQtr6JuA*
Introduction: 8 measures
Measures:

FIRST STEP
Moving CCW

1   Step on R (ct 1), scuff L (ct &)
       Step on L (ct 2), scuff R (ct &)
       Russian two-step

2   R (ct 1), L (ct &), R (ct 2), scuff L (ct &)
3-4   Repeat meas 1-2 opp ft
5   Facing ctr: Step R to the right side (ct 1)
       Step on L behind R (ct &)
       Step slightly to right on R (ct 2)
       Tap L heel next to R (ct &)
6   Repeat meas 5 opp ft
       Into ctr
7   Repeat meas 1
8   Run 4 small step forward on R (ct 1), L(ct &), R (ct 2), L (ct &)

SECOND STEP
Syncopated step

1   Step on R (ct 1), tap L heel to side of R, no weight (ct &)
       Lift L (ct 2), tap L heel in place (ct &)
2   Repeat meas 1 opp ft
3-4   Repeat meas 1-2
       Reel back
5   Lift R, hook it behind L (ct 1), step on R (ct &)
       Lift L, hook it behind R (ct 2), step on L (ct &)
6   Repeat meas 5
7   repeat meas 1
8   In place, light stamps: L(ct 1), R (ct &), L (ct 2)

Note: "Oy, Baboushka" is same choreography as Jest Vino only "Oy, Baboushka" is faster.

OY, PRI LOUZHKA (Russia)

Dance Meaning: On the Meadow
Pronunciation: Oye, Pree Louzhka ("zh" pronounced as in mea<u>s</u>ure)
Choreography: By Jim Gold using traditional steps from Russia
Music: Ensemble Podvorye
Formation: Open circle
Meter: 4/4
Jim Gold YouTube video: *https://www.youtube.com/watch?v=nRoAH8woN2E*
Introduction: 4 measures
Measures:

FIRST STEP

Stiff-kneed gliding walk, CCW, fists on hips
R (ct 1), L (ct 2), R (ct 3), L (ct 4)

2-4   Repeat meas 1 3x

Sun rise and set step

5-6   Repeat meas 1-2, hands open, fingers together, arms trace ascent of sun moving in 3/4 circle from left to right.

7-8   Repeat meas 1-2 with arms moving in opposite direction tracing descent of sun.

Gallop step, fists on hips

9-12   Step forward on R bending knee and dipping slightly (ct 1)
Straighten both knees, bring L next to R (ct &)
Repeat 7x.

SECOND STEP

Face ctr

1   Step R to right (ct 1), bring L next to R (ct 2)
Step R to right (ct 3), bring L next to R (ct 4)

2   Repeat meas 1 opp ft and opp dir

4 pas de bas

3   Step on R (ct 1), step on L in front of R (ct &)
Step on R in place (ct 2)
Step on L (ct 3), step on R in front of L (ct &)
Step on L in place (ct 2)

4   Repeat meas 3

5   Lifts: Step on R (ct 1), lift L (ct 2)
Step on L (ct 3), lift R (ct 4)

6   Step on R (ct 1),

Cross L over R (ct 2), snap R foot to L foot (ct 3-4)

4 push steps: moving left, CW

7   Push off on R ft and fall on L ft (ct 1)

Close R to L (ct 2)

Push off on R ft and fall on L ft (ct 3)

Close R to L (ct 4)

8   Repeat meas 7

THIRD STEP

Step-lifts into ctr

1   Raise R hand high: Step on R (ct 1), lift L (ct 2)

Step on L (ct 3), lift R (ct 4)

2   Repeat meas 1

Rida step out of circle, half turn left, left shoulder facing out of circle

3   Cross R over L (ct 1), bring L to side of R (ct 2)

cross R over L (ct 3), bring L to side of R (ct 4)

4   Cross R over L (ct 1), bring L to side of R (ct 2), cross R over L(ct 3)

Half turn to face CCW, step on L (ct 4).

PAK SUM PIYAN (Bulgaria)

Dance Meaning: Again We Drink
Pronunciation: Pak Sum Peeyan
Choreography: By Jim Gold using traditional steps from East Bulgaria and
        Macedonia
Music: Pak Sum Piyan: Peroun
Formation: Open circle, arms in W position.
Jim Gold YouTube video: *https://www.youtube.com/watch?v=sDwMmGO2eX0*
Meter: 7/8: slow/quick/quick: s, q, q
Introduction: Five measures.

FIRST STEP
3-step grapevine and "crossing" two-step
1   Step on R to rt side (s), step on L behind R (q), bring R next to L (q)
2   Step L across and in front of R (s), bring R next to L (q), cross L in front of R (q)

Back pas de bas
3   Step on R (s), step L behind R (q), step on R in place (q)
4   Step on L (ct s), step on R behind L (ct q), step on L in place (q)
5-7   Repeat meas 1-3
8   Step fwd on L (ct s), lift R (ct q, q)
9-14 Repeat meas 1-6
        Turn CW
15   Step R (s), step L (q), step R (q),
16   Step on L (s), step on R (q, q)

SECOND STEP
Balance step: Lift and Hold
1   Step fwd on L, lift R leg in front of L and hold (s, q. q)
2   Swing R leg behind L knee and hold (s, q, q)
3   Swing and lift R leg in front of L and hold (s, q, q)
4   Step to rt side on R (s), bring L next to R (q, q)
5   Step fwd on R, lift L leg and hold (s, q, q)
6   Swing L leg behind R knee and hold (s, q, q)
7   Swing and lift L leg in front of R (s), step on L to left (q), step R behind L (q)
8   Step on L next to R (s), step on R(q, q)
9-15 Repeat meas 1-7
16   Step on L next to R (s), tch R next to L (q, q)

ORDER OF STEPS
1. First Step: 1x, Second Step: 1x

PAVLE MOU PIE (BULGARIA)

Dance Meaning: Paul Sings to me
Pronunciation: Pavle moo pee'a
Choreography: by Jim Gold in Bulgarian folk dance style
Music: Pirin Ensemble
Formation: Open circle, arms in V position
Meter: 2/4
Jim Gold YouTube Video: *http://bit.ly/2nnnLCN*
Introduction: 8 or 16 meas
Measures:

First Version

FIRST STEP
Basic hora

1	Step R to rt (ct 1), cross L over R (ct 2)
2	Step R (ct 1), lift L (ct 2)
3	Step on L (ct 1), lift R (ct 2)
4-24	Repeat meas 1-3 7x

SECOND STEP
Pravo and grapevine
Moving diag right into ctr

1	R (ct 1), L (ct &), R (ct 2)
2	L (ct 1)

Move diag rt out of ctr

R (ct 2), step on L (ct &)

3	R (ct 1), L (ct 2)
4-6	Diag right out of ctr, Repeat meas 1-3

4-step grapevine

7	Step R to rt (ct 1), step L front of R (ct 2)
8	Step R to rt side of R (ct 3), step L behind R (ct 4)
9-14	Repeat meas 1-6 of SECOND STEP

Pravo and two stamps

15	Step on R (ct 1), light stamp on L (ct 2)
16	Step on L (ct 1), light stamp on R (ct 2)

ORDER OF STEPS
1. First Step: 1x, Second Step: 1x

PLATKY (RUSSIA)

Dance Meaning: Plaited or braid
Pronunciation: Plat-kY (accent last syllable)
Music: The Maydan: Kazachiv Ensemble of Song and Dance
Choreography: By Jim Gold in Russian folk dance style
Formation: Open circle. Hands held down in V formation
Meter: 4/4
Jim Gold YouTube video: *https://www.youtube.com/watch?v=8dSJQ09x3MU*
Introduction: 2 measures
Measures:

FIRST STEP
Moving to the right, CCW: Russian two-step, and walk

1   Step forward on R (ct 1), bring L behind R (ct &)
       Step R forward (ct 2), brush left foot forward pointing toe (ct &)
       Step forward on L (ct 3), bring R behind L (ct &)
       Step L forward (ct 4), brush right foot forward pointing toe (ct &)

2   **Walk 4 steps in LOD**
       R (ct 1), L (ct 2), R (ct 3), L (ct 4)

3-4   Repeat meas 1-2

SECOND STEP
Toe-heel-lift-push step, face fwd

1   Touch R toe to right bending right knee towards left knee (ct 1),
       Touch R heel in same spot (ct &)
       Lift R ft in front of left shin with R foot parallel to left shin (ct 2)
       Push R ft to right (ct &)
       Step R ft to right (ct 3), close L ft next to R (ct &)
       Step R ft to rt (ct 4), close L ft next to R with no weight on L (ct &)

2   Repeat meas 1 cts 1-3 opp dir and opp ft,
       Step L ft to lft(ct 4), push R ft fwd(ct &)

3   **Gliding rida to left, CW, stay on toes**
       Step R ft in front of L (ct 1), step L to left side behind R (ct &)
       Repeat (ct 1 &) 3x.

4   **8-step grapevine to left, CW, stay on toes**
       Step R in front of L (ct 1), step L to left side of R (ct &)
       Step R behind L (ct 2), L to left side of R (ct &)
       Step R in front of L (ct 3), step L to left side of R (ct &)
       Step R behind L as you turn body CCW with L shoulder
       facing ctr (ct 4)
       Step on L in front of R (ct &)

THIRD STEP

   Three-sided rectangle step
   8 gliding steps into ctr: 1st side of rectangle
   Style: On toes. left shoulder facing ctr

1   Cross R over L (ct 1), step L behind R (ct &)
       Repeat (ct 1&) 3x.
       8 gliding steps to left. CW: 2nd side of rectangle
2   Cross R over L (ct 1), step L behind R (ct &)
       Repeat (ct 1 &) 3x
       Toe-heel-lift-push-step
3-4   Repeat meas 1-2 of Second Step
       8 gliding steps to left. CW: 2nd side of rectangle
5   Cross R over L (ct 1), step L behind R (ct &)
       Repeat (ct 1 &) 3x
       6 gliding steps back: 3rd side of rectangle
6   Cross R over L (ct 1), step on L behind R (ct &)
       Cross R over L (ct 2), step on L behind R (ct &)
       Cross R over L (ct 3), step on L behind R (ct &)
       Step back on R facing ctr (ct 4)
       Step L next to R (ct &) Completes three-sided rectangle
       Toe-heel-cross-push step of meas 1 from Second Step
7   Touch R toe to right bending right knee towards left knee (ct 1)
       Touch R heel in same spot (ct &)
       Lift R ft in front of left shin with R foot parallel to left (ct 2)
       Push R ft to right (ct &), face ctr step R ft to right (ct 3)
       Close L ft next to R (ct), step R ft to rt(ct 4)
       Close L ft next to R L(ct &)
8   **3 reels back**
       Lift R leg (ct 1), step on R ft behind L (ct)
       Lift L leg (ct 2), step on L ft behind R (ct &)
       Lift R leg (ct 3), step on R ft behind L (ct &)
       Step on L ft next to R (ct 4).
       Repeat entire pattern twice

Dance notes by Jim Gold presented by Jim Gold at the Florida Folk Dance Camp, February 2004.

POGONISHTE KRUJA (Albania)

Dance Meaning: Pogonishte from Kruja
Choreography: By Jim Gold in Albanian folk dance style
Music: The Dirge of Permet, Lyra CD, Laver Barlou clarinet.
      Editors: Alkis Raftis and Vangelis Roubas
Formation: Open circle, hands W position
Meter: 4/4
Notes on Pogonishte: by Cees Hillebrand. See bottom of page
Jim Gold YouTube video: *https://www.youtube.com/watch?v=r_hLICgOxYA*
Introduction: 12 meas
Measures:

FIRST STEP
    Basic Pogonishte step 8x, moving CCW
    Upbeat; lift L (ct 4)

1	Step L (ct 1), step R (ct 2), step L (ct 3), lift R (ct 4)
2	Step R (ct 1), step L behind R (ct 2), step R to rt (ct 3)
	Lift and cross L in front of R (ct 4)
3-16	Repeat meas 1-2 8x

SECOND STEP
    Sway cross step

1	Lift L (ct 1), step L (ct 2), step R (ct 3), step L (ct 4)

    Crossing step
    Moving in to ctr of circle , 3 sway cross steps

2	Step R to rt (ct 1), step L to lft (ct 2), cross R over L (ct 3-4)
3	Step L to lft (ct 1), step R to rt (ct 2), cross L over R (ct 3-4)
4-5	Repeat meas 2-3 1x

    Moving our of ctr, 3 sway cross steps

6	Step R to rt (ct 1), step L to lft (ct 2), cross R over L (ct 3-4)
7	Step L to lft (ct 1), step R to rt (ct 2), cross L over R (ct 3-4)
8-11	Repeat meas 6-7 2x
12	Full turn: R (ct 1), L (ct 2), R (ct 3-4)

ORDER OF STEPS
1. First Step: 8x 2. Second Step: 1x

Notes on Pogonishte

In Albania there is a region named Pogon—south of Zagoria, a bit south-east of Gjirokastër, dand east of Libohova.

Is it often said that the name Pogonishte is the same as the dance Poginisios from Greece. Actually Pogon is a valley between two mountain ranges (Mali i Buretos on the west side, and Mali I Nemerçkës on the east, ranging from north to south) that has its northern part in Albania and its southern in Greece, down to Delvinaki, widening as the valley mobes southward.

The name comes in fact from the region, not from the village of Pogoni as is often claimed. Pogoni is a cluster of villages in Greece of a much later date, and the actual village, Pogoniani, was named much later; it had formerly been known as Vostina.

To make all this even more complicated, all the villages in the Albanian Pogon region have Greek inhabitants except for one, which is inhabited by Albanians. It is said that the Greek government decided to establish a Pogoni "city" in order to be able to claim that the Albanian territory belonged to Greece. I have an opinion on this political aspect; it might simply have been made up, for obvious reasons.

The word *Pogon* as an *etymological* concept differs. Look at the surrounding regions: Zagoria is of Slavic origin, are Corovoda (Crno Voda, "black water") in the more northern region, Poliçan (Po–liçan), and many more examples. Pogon can be found in the Polish, Serbian, and Slovenian languages and is translated as "drive" or "power" or "chase –pursuit". But there is no further connection. The Bulgarian book on Slavic names in Albania refers to Zagoria and others, but makes no mention of Pogon. So I do not dare to assume that connection as a true one. It is not known in Macedonian and Bulgarian language.

The point is that almost all the regions with Slavic names in the south are occupied by Greek immigrants who worked on the fields. The villages of the Dropulli region have names like Lazarat, Derviçan, Goranxi and Goricë, but all are inhabited by Greek immigrants.

—*Cees Hillebrand*

POLEGNALA E TODORA (BULGARIA)

Dance Meaning: Todora is lying (under a tree)
Pronunciation: Po leg NALA eh to DOR a
Choreography: Jim Gold in Bulgarian folk dance style
Music: Filip Kutev Choir
Formation: Open circle, arms in W position
Meter: 8/8: 1-2, 1-2-3, 1-2-3. qq s s
Jim Gold YouTube video: *http://bit.ly/2qUWSLk*
Choir Singing: Filip Kutev Choir
Introduction: 4 measures
Measures:

FIRST STEP
Face ctr
Two "quite sashay" 2-steps, 8 step grapevine CCW

1   Step R to r (q), close L to R (q), step R to rt (s), cross L over R (s)
2   Repeat meas 1
     8 step grapevine
3   Step R to rt (q), L behind R (q), step R to rt (s), cross L over R (s)
4   Repeat meas 3

SECOND STEP
Face ctr, Lesnoto lift. CCW

1   Step R to rt (qq), lift L (s), cross L over R, step on L (s)
2   Repeat meas 1
     Ctr and back
3   Step fwd on R (q), bring L next to R (q), step fwd on R (s), step fwd on L (s)
4   Step back on R (q), bring L next to R (q), step back on R (s)
     Step back on L, tch rt toe to L (s)
5-8 Repeat meas 1-4

ORDER OF STEPS
After intro
1. First Step: 1x, Second Step: 2x
2 to end: First Step 2x, Second step 2x

Polegnala ye Todora

*(This is a folk song from Bulgaria about a girl called Tudora.
Latin Transliteration.)*

Polegnala ye Tudora,
Moma Tudoro, Tudoro x2
Pod durvo pod maslinova
Moma Tudoro, Tudoro x2

Poveya vetrets gornenets,
Moma Tudoro, Tudoro x2
Ot kurshi klonka maslina,
Moma Tudoro, Tudoro
Che si Tudora subudi
Moma Tudoro, Tudoro

A tya muse lyuta surdi,
Moma Tudoro, Tudoro x2
Vetre le nenaveniko,
Moma Tudoro, Tudoro
Sega li naide de veyesh,
Moma Tudoro, Tudoro

Sladka si sunya sunuvakh
Moma Tudoro, Tudoro x2
Che mi doshlo purvo libe
Moma Tudoro, Tudoro
I doneslo pustra kitka,
Moma Tudoro, Tudoro
I doneslo pustra kitka,
Moma Tudoro, Tudoro
A na kitka zlaten pursten
Moma Tudoro, Tudoro.

Original lyrics in the Cyrillic alphabet:

Полегнала е Тодора,
мома Тодоро, Тодоро,
под дърво, под маслиново,
мома Тодоро, Тодоро.

Повея ветрец горнинец,
мома Тодоро, Тодоро,
откърши клонка маслина,
мома Тодоро, Тодоро,
че си Тодора събуди,
мома Тодоро, Тодоро.

А тя му се люто сърди,
мома Тодоро, Тодоро,
"Ветре ле, ненавейнико,
мома Тодоро, Тодоро,
сега ли найде да вееш!"
мома Тодоро, Тодоро.

"Сладка си съня сънувах,
мома Тодоро, Тодоро,
че ми дошло първо либе,
мома Тодоро, Тодоро,
и донесло пъстра китка,
мома Тодоро, Тодоро.
И донесло пъстра китка,
мома Тодоро, Тодоро,
а на китка златен пръстен!"
мома Тодоро, Тодоро.

Translation:

Tudora is lying under a tree, an olive tree. The moutain
breeze gently blows and breaks a twig off the olive tree. Tudora
is awakened. She is very angry at the breeze that blows tirelessly.
"Why are you blowing just now? I was dreaming my first love
came, and brought me a small colorful bouquet. He brought me
a small bouquet and on it was a gold ring.

POSLOUSHAITE PATRIOTI (BULGARIA)

Dance Meaning: Listen Patriots
Pronunciation: Pa-SLOO-shayte Patri-O-ti
Choreography: By Jim Gold using traditional steps from Bulgaria and Macedonia
Source: Koprivshtitsa Folk Festival 2000 in Bulgaria
Music: Posloushaite Patriot Peroun
Formation: Open circle, arms in W position
Meter: 7/8: slow/quick/quick: s, q, q
Jim Gold YouTube video: *http://bit.ly/2fFVIvC*
Introduction: Long flute sound, then 8 measure intro
Measures:

FIRST STEP
Hora step

1	Step R to right (s), left in front (q, q)
2	Step R to right (s), step L behind R (q ,q)
3	Step on R (s), lift L (q, q)
4	Step L (s), lift R (q, q)
5-16	Repeat meas 1-4 3x

SECOND STEP
Patrioti Step

1	Facing ctr: Step forward on R (s)
	Bring L ft behind R knee (q, q)
2	Step back on L(s), lift R leg high (q, q)
3	Hook R to right in reel step (s)
	Lock R ft behind L knee (q, q)
4	Step back on R (s), step on L next to R (q, q)

3 back pas de bas

5	Step L to left (s), step R behind L (q), step on L in place (q)
6	Repeat meas 5 opp dir and opp ft
7	Repeat meas 5

THIRD STEP
Walk to right, CCW

1	R (s), L (q), R (q)
2	L (s), R (q), L(q)

Grapevine 3 to the left, CW, crossing step

3	Step R over left (s), L besides R (q), Step R behind L (q)

Crossing step

4   Step on L in place (s), cross R in front of L (q), step on L in place (q)

5-7   Repeat meas 1-3

8   Step on L (s), touch R toe next to L instep (q, q)

9-16   Repeat Third Step.

POZDRAV (BULGARIA)

Dance Meaning: Greetings!
Pronunciation: Pozdrav
Choreography: by Jim Gold in Macedonia-Bulgarian folk dance style
Music: Makeonska Pesni: Stoyan Djhadjhev
Formation: Open circle, hands in W position
Meter: 9/8: quick/quick/quick/quick, slow: q, q, q, qs
Jim Gold YouTube video: https://www.youtube.com/watch?v=YmTuRIsPyrM
Introduction: 8 measures
Measures:

FIRST STEP

Moving to Rt: Face LOD. CWW, hands in W position

1   Step R to rt (q), step L behind R (q), step R to rt turn to face LOD (q)
    Hop on R(q), step fwd on L(s)

2   Moving CCW: Step R (q), step L (q), step R (q), tch L fwd (qs)
    Moving reverse LOD:

3   L (q), R (q), L (q), face ctr: tch R in place (qs)
    Crossing step, still facing ctr.

4   Cross R over L (q), step L next to R (q), cross R over L(q)
    Step on L next to R (qs)

5   Crossing step: Cross R in front of L(q), step on L in place(q)
    Step on R next to L(q), step on L (qs)
    Into ctr
    Hands start moving down to V position

6   R (q), L (q), R (q), hands return to W position, tch L fwd (qs)
    Back out of ctr: hands start moving down to V position

7   L (q), R (q), L (q), hands return to W position, R (qs)

SECOND STEP (Optional)

Into ctr
Hands moving down to V position

1   Step R into ctr (q), step L (q), step on R (q)
    Hands to W position, hop on R (q), step fwd on L (qs)
    Continue int ctr: Hands moving down to V position

2   R (q), L (q), R (q), hands return to W position, tch L fwd (qs)

3   **Back out from ctr: Hands remain in W position**
    L (q), R (q), L (q), R (qs)

4 Cross R over L (q), step L next to R (q)
  Cross R over L (q), step on L next to R (qs)

5 Cross R over L (½ q), step L next to R (½ q)
  Cross R over L (½ q), step on L next to R (½ q)
  Cross R over L (½ q), step L next to R (½ q)
  Cross R over L (½ q), step on L next to R (½ qs)

6 **Crossing step:** Cross R in front of L (q), step on L in place (q)
  Step on R next to L (q), step on L next to R (qs)

7 Step on R (q), stamp lightly on L next to R (q)
  Step on L (q), stamp lightly on R next to lft (qs).

ORDER OF STEPS
First Step: 2x, Second step: 2x

PRAVO HORO IVAN (BULGARIA)

Dance meaning: Straight, to the right
Pronunciation: PRA-vo Ho-RO I-VAN
Choreography: Traditional
Music: Folklore Gems: Ivan Kirev Accordion
Formation: Line, arms in V position
Meter: 2/4 or 6/8
Jim Gold YouTube video: *https://www.youtube.com/watch?v=h_VlFdBDfSQ*
Introduction: 10 measures
Measures:

Basic Pravo step
Diagonally into ctr
1   R (ct 1), L (ct 2)
2   R (ct 1-2)
3   Step on L (ct 1-2)
4-6   Repeat meas 1-3 diag bkwd.
Kazanluk variation
1   Sway right (ct 1), sway left (ct 2)
2   Step forward on R and dip(1-2)
3   Step on L (ct 1), lightly stamp R next to L (ct 2)
4   Step back on R (ct 1), step on L next to R (ct 2)
5   Step back on R (ct 1-2)
6   Step back on left (ct 1-2)

Presented by Jim Gold at the Florida Folk Dance Camp, February 2004.

PRODOMENI AGAPI (GREECE)

Dance Meaning: Betrayal of Love
Pronunciation: Pro-do-MENI A-GA-pi
Choreography: By Jim Gold in Greek folk dance style
Music: Mikos Thedorakis
Formation: Open Circle, arms in W position
Meter: 4/4
Jim Gold YouTube video: *https://www.youtube.com/watch?v=N28V4vrmMxo*
Introduction: 4 measures
Measures:

FIRST STEP

Grapevine, two lifts, two sides
Grapevine

1 Step to right on R (ct 1), cross left in front over R (ct 2)
   Step to right on R (ct 3), cross left in front over R (ct 4)
   Lifts

2 Step on R (ct 1), lift L(ct 2), step on L (ct 3), lift R(ct 4)
   Sides

3 Step to right on R (ct 1), cross left behind R (ct 2)
   Step on R (ct 3), Lift L (ct 4)

4 Repeat meas 3: opp dir and opp ft.
   Improvised and optional turns called by leader, as are inspirational cries of "opa" or "giro."

ORDER OF STEPS

Dance first step 6 times, middle break: 3 crossing steps, then begin First Step.
Dance it 8 more times.

RAITI B'CHALOM (Israel)

Dance Meaning: I Saw In A Dream
Pronunciation: Raeetee BaHalom
Choreography: by Jim Gold in Yemenite folk dance style
Music: L'Haiti Timan sung by Zion Golan
Formation: Open Circle, free hands
Yemenite Style: Bouncy, waves of sand, (head) swaying, ("bobbing"), up feel:
"Dancing up to God"
Meter: 2/4
Jim Gold YouTube video: *https://www.youtube.com/watch?v=p3ePk-pCx-4*
Introduction: 16
Measures:

FIRST STEP

Face ct: Right Yemenite

1   Sway rt (ct 1), sway lft (ct &), cross R over L (ct 2)

Left Yemenite (LRL)

2   Repeat meas 1 opp. ft

3   Sway fwd on R (ct 1), Sway back on L (ct 2)

4   Yemenite fwd (RLR), with rt hand held higher in Yemenite "wave"

5   Yemenite back (LRL), with rt hand held higher Yemenite "wave"

6   Yemenite R (RLR) and hold (stop) on R with no weight

7-11   Repeat meas 1-2

12   Yemenite turn to left (RLR)

SECOND STEP

1   Face ctr: Yem R (RLR),

2   Yem L(LRL)

       Yem back (RLR)

Step back and into ctr 5 steps

3   Step back on R (ct 1), step L next to R (ct &), now step on R as you make 1/4 turn rt. (L shldr faces ctr (ct 2).) cross wrists for fingers snap Yem. style. Step L behind R (ct &)

4   Cross R over L (ct 1), step L behind R (ct &)

       Cross and step on R (ct 2)

5   Facing CW: Yem L (LRL)

6   Yem R (RLR)

Step back and out of ctr 5 steps

7   Still facing CW, step back on L (ct 1), step R next to L (ct &)

Cross L over R: Still face CW, R shldr faces out of ctr, **cross wrists for fingers snap Yem. style (ct 2)**, step R behind L (ct &)

8   Cross L over R (ct 1), step on R (ct &)

Cross L over R (ct 2), make 1/4 turn to face ctr (ct &).

THIRD STEP

1   Face ctr, step on R to rt, arms out parallel to floor (ct 1), Cross L over R, cross wrists and snap fingers, Yem snap (ct 2)

2   Repeat meas 1

3-4   Repeat meas, 1-2

2 Grapevines to rt: (Yem style: "rise and dip").

5   Step to rt on R, rise (ct 1), step on L in front of R, dip (ct &)

Step to rt on R, rise (ct 2), step on L behind R, dip (ct &)

6   Repeat meas 5

7-11   Repeat meas 1-5

12   Step to rt on R, rise (ct 1), step on L behind R, dip (ct &)

Bring R next to L (ct 2)

ORDER OF STEPS

1. First Step: 1x, Second Step: 1x, Third Step: 1x
2. First Step: 1x, Second Step: 1x, Third Step: 1x
3. First Step: 1x, Second Step: 1x, Third Step: 4x
4. First Step: 1x, Second Step: 1x, Third Step: 1x
5. First Step: 1x, Second Step: 1x, Third Step: ½

REEL DU PANIER (CANADA, NOVA SCOTIA)

Dance Meaning: Basket Reel
Pronunciation: Reel doo pan-YEI
Choreography: By Jim Gold using folk dance elements from Cajun/French Canadian, Bulgaria (Pravo), Croatia (lame duck step), and Hungary (Pontozo) dance styles.
Style: Fusion style. Free hands. Arms down
Music: Barachois: French Cajun Band
Formation: Open circle, hold hands, arms down in V position. On fourth step, hands free, arms held high, snap fingers.
Meter: 2/4
Jim Gold YouTube video: *https://www.youtube.com/watch?v=iL383G364MQ*
Introduction: 8 measures
Measures:

FIRST STEP

Into ctr diag right (Canadian Pravo)

1   2 two-steps: L (ct 1), R (ct &), L (ct 2)
2   Repeat meas 1 using opp ft

Move diag right out of circle

3   Cross L over R (ct 1), step R to the right side (ct 2)
4   Repeat meas 3
5-6 Repeat meas 1-2

Move diag right with cross step out of circle

7   cross L over R (ct 1), step R to the right side (ct &), cross L over R (ct 2)
     Step R to the right side (ct &)
8   Repeat measure 7

SECOND STEP

Moving CCW (Croatian lame duck)

1   Step on L (ct 1), lift R in a sweep step (ct 2)
2   Step on R (ct 1), L behind R (ct &), step on R (ct 2)
3-4 Repeat meas 1-2
5-6 Repeat meas 1-2
7   Step on L (ct 1), lift R in a big sweep step, quarter turn, face ctr (ct 2)
8   Step on R (ct 1), step on (L ct 2)

THIRD STEP

Four clog-shuffle steps

1   Brush R toe forward (ct ½ &)

    Brush R toe back (ct ½ &), step on R ft (ct 1)

    Brush L toe forward (ct ½ &)

    Brush L toe back (ct ½ &), step on L ft (ct 2)

2   Brush R toe forward (ct ½ &)

    Brush R toe back (ct ½ &), step on R ft (ct 1)

    Brush L toe forward (ct ½ &)

    Brush L toe back (ct ½ &), step on L ft (ct 2)

3   8-step crossing (Canadian Cherkassia step)

    Cross R front of L (ct 1), step on L in   place (ct &)

    Step on R to side of L (ct 2), step on L in place (ct &)

4   Repeat measure 3

5-6   Repeat meas 1-2 (clogging step)

7-step crossing: (Cherkessia step)

7   Cross R front of L (ct 1), step on L in place (ct &)

    Step on R to side of L (ct 2), step on L in place (ct &)

8   Cross R front of L(ct 1), step on L in place (ct &), Step on R (ct 2)

FOURTH STEP

French Canadian Pontozo Step: Arms held high, snap fingers

1   Step slightly forward on L (ct 1)

    Lift R with ronde de jambe turning R hip slightly forward (ct 2)

2   Stamp R heel forward (no weight) with R toe facing diag left (ct 1)

    Stamp R heel forward (no weight) with R toe facing diag right (ct &)

    Stamp R heel forward (no weight) with R toe facing diag left (ct 2)

    Stamp R heel forward (no weight) with R toe facing diag right (ct &)

3   Step forward on R(ct 1), lift L with ronde de jambe turning

    left hip slightly forward (ct 2)

4   Repeat of meas 2 with opp ft

    Stamp L heel forward (no weight) with left toe facing diag

    right (ct 1)

    Stamp L heel forward (no weight) with left toe facing diag left (ct &)

    Stamp L heel forward (no weight) with L toe facing diag right (ct 2)

    Stamp L heel forward (no weight) with L toe facing diag left (ct &)

5-6   Repeat meas 1-2

7 step grapevine to left, CW

7   Step on R in front of L (ct 1), step on L to left side of R (ct &)

    Step R behind L (ct 2), step L to left side of R (ct &)

8   Step on R in front of L (ct 1), step L to left side of R (ct &)
       Step R next to L (ct 2)

ORDER OF STEPS
First Step: 2x, Second Step: 1x
Third Step: 1x, Fourth Step: 1x
Then repeat pattern until end

RUSSIAN ROUND (Russia)

Choreography: By Jim Gold using folk dance elements from traditional
    Russian steps.
Music: Barinya: Russian Folk Dances presented by Alexandru David "Bielolitsa,
Krieglolitsa"
Meter: 4/4
Jim Gold YouTube video: *https://www.youtube.com/watch?v=8sHLx-5KgYg&t=4s*
Formation: Three concentric circles. Steps given are for inner circle only/
    Step Tossing: Inner circle dances first step, then passes or "tosses" it to the
    second circle, second circle the step, then tosses steps to third circle. This
    process continues throughout the dance.
Order:
    1. **Inner circle begins with step one.** Second and third circle remain
        motionless.
    2. **Inner circle begins step two.** Second circle begins step one. Third circle
        remains motionless.
    3. **Inner circle begins step three.** Second circle begins step two. Third circle
        begins step one. Etc.

Introduction: 4 measures
Measures:

FIRST STEP
Walking step: 15 Walking steps CCW

1	Step R (ct 1), Step L (ct 2), step R (ct 3), step, L (ct 4)
2	Repeat meas 1
3	Repeat meas 1
4	Step R (ct 1), step L (ct 2), step R and face ctr (ct 3), touch L to R (ct 4)
5-8	Repeat meas 1-4 opp dir and opp ft

SECOND STEP
8 Side Steps, CCW

1	Face ctr, step R to the right (ct 1), bring L next to R (ct 2) Step R to the right (ct 3), bring L next to R (ct 4)
2-3	Repeat meas 1 2x
4	Step R to the right (ct 1), bring L next to R (ct 2) Step R to the right (ct 3), touch L next to R (ct 4)
5-8	Repeat meas 1-4 opp. dir

THIRD STEP

Walks and turns

8 quick-walk steps circling to the right, CCW

1   Step R (ct 1), step L (ct &), step R (ct 2), step L (ct &)

     step R (ct 3), step L (ct &), step R (ct 4), step L (ct &)

8 turning steps to the right, hold R hand in air

2   Step R (ct 1), step L (ct &), step R (ct 2), step L (ct &)

     Step R (ct 3), step L (ct &), step (ct 4), step L (ct &)

3   Repeat meas 1

7 turning steps to the right

4   Step R (ct 1), step L (ct &), step R (ct 2), step L (ct &)

     Step R (ct 3), step L (ct &), step R (ct 4), touch L to R (ct &)

5-8 Repeat meas 1-4 opp dir and opp ft, opp hand (L hand) raised in turn.

FOURTH STEP

Gliding step

Stiff kneed walk, gliding step style: 31 gliding steps CCW

1   Step R (ct 1), step L (ct &), step R (ct 2), step L (ct &)

     Step R (ct 3), step L (ct &), step R (ct 4), step L (ct &)

2-3 Repeat meas 2x

4   Step R (ct 1), step L (ct &), step R (ct 2), step L (ct &)

     Step R (ct 3), step L (ct &), step R (ct 2) touch L to R (ct &)

5-8 Repeat meas 1-4 in opp dir and opp ft

FIFTH STEP

Russian Side Steps: Right hand behind head Russian style. Left fist on hip.

1-4 Repeat Second Step

-8   Repeat meas 1-4 opp dir and opp ft

SIXTH STEP

1-8 Repeat First Step

SEVENTH STEP

1-8 Repeat Fourth Step

EIGHTH STEP

8 waving-arms steps

1-4 Repeat Second Step with arms moving side to side like a windshield wiper.

5-8   Repeat meas 1-4 opp dir
       Add waving handkerchiefs.

NINTH STEP

1-4   Repeat Third Step
       At final turn, inner circle members, holding handkerchiefs in R hand,
       create wreath of handkerchiefs by offering (putting) their hand-held
       handkerchiefs into center of the circle.

SBOGAM, MILA (Bulgaria)

Dance Meaning: I Meet my Dear One
Pronunciation: Sbogam, Mila
Choreography: by Jim Gold in Macedonian folk dance style
Music: Stoyan Djadjev, Makedonski Pesni
Formation: Open circle, arms in V position
Meter: 4/4
Jim Gold YouTube video: *https://www.youtube.com/watch?v=n7ijoWORbYI*
Introduction: 12 measures
Measures:

FIRST STEP
> **Slower music, lean-heavy step**
> **Facing LOD. walk to rt**

1   Step to R (ct 1), step on L (ct2), step on R (ct &)
          Step on L (ct 3), face ctr, step R and lean- heavy to rt (ct 4)

2   Step on L (ct 1), cross R in front of L (ct &)
          Step on L in place (ct 2), step on R next to L(ct &)
          Step on L in place (ct 3), Lift R (ct &, ct 4)

3-8   Repeat meas 1-2, 3x

SECOND STEP
> **Music a bit faster: Sides and into ctr**

1   Step R to rt (ct 1), place L next to R (ct 2)
          Step R to rt (ct 3), place L next to R (ct 4)

2   Step R to rt (ct 1), place L next to R (ct 2)
          Step R to rt (ct 3), place L next to R (ct 4)
> **Grapevine**

3   Step R to rt (ct 1), step L in front of R (ct 2)
          Step R to rt (ct 3), step L behind R (ct 4)

4   Step R to rt (ct 1), lift L (ct 2)
          Step L to left (ct 3), lift R (ct 4)
> **Moving into ctr**

5   Step R fwd (ct 1), bring L next to R (ct 2), step R fwd (ct 3-4)

6   Step L fwd (ct 1), bring R next to L (ct 2), step L fwd (ct 4)
> **Moving diag out of circle**

7   Cross R over L (ct 1), step L next to R (ct 2)
          Cross R over L (ct 2),step L next to R (ct 3), cross R over L (ct 4)

8   Cross R over L (ct 1),step L next to R (ct 2), step L next to R (ct 3)

Cross R over L (ct 4), step on L behind R (ct 4)

Face ctr

9   Step R to rt (ct 1), place L next to R (ct 2), step R to rt (ct 3), place L next to R(ct 4)

Lifts

10   Step R to rt(ct 1), lift L (ct 2), step L to left (ct 3), lift R (ct 4)

Moving fwd and back:

11   Step fwd into circle: R fwd (ct 1), bring L next to R (ct 2), step R fwd (ct 3-4)

12   Step back on L (ct 1), bring R next to L (ct 2), step back on L (ct 3-4)

SBORENSKO HORO (BULGARIA)

Dance Meaning: Meeting dance
Pronunciation: SBOR-ensko Hor-O
Choreography: By Jim Gold in Bulgarian folk dance style
Style: North Bulgarian folk dance style
Music: Folk Dances from North Bulgaria: Yanko Zhelyazkov, Accordion
Formation: Line, belt or low hand hold, V position
Meter: 4/4
Jim Gold YouiTube video: *https://www.youtube.com/watch?v=kaVYxUDm1Do*
Introduction: 4 measures
Measures:

FIRST STEP

Into ct: Walk 3 steps and lift

1   Step R fwd (ct 1), step L fwd (ct 2), step R fwd (ct 3), lift L (ct 4)

Back out of ctr

2   Step L back (ct 1), step R back (ct 2), step L back (ct 3), Lift R (ct 4)

3   Step on R (ct 1), lift L (ct 2), step L (ct 3), lift R (ct 4)

4   Step R (ct 1), lift L (ct 2), step on L(ct 3)
      Stamp on R diag left (ct &), step on R diag right (ct 4)

-6   Repeat measures 1-2

North Bulgarian Alunelul-type step

7   Facing ctr step on R in place (ct 1), stamp L next to R (ct &)
      Step on L (ct 2), stamp R next to L (ct &)
      Step on R (ct 3), stamp on L next to R (ct &), stamp on L next to R
      (ct 4)

8   Repeat meas 7 with opp ft

SECOND STEP

Face ctr. Moving to the right, CCW

1   Step R to right (ct 1), step L behind R (ct 2)
      Step R to rt(ct 3), step L behind R (ct 4)

2   Step R to rt (ct 1), step L behind R (ct 2), step R to rt (ct 3)
      Stamp on L heel next to R (ct 4)

3-4   Repeat meas 1-2 opp ft and opp dir

5   Repeat meas 1

4 quick ones

6   Step R to right (ct 1), step L behind R (ct &)
      Step R to right (ct 2), step L behind R (ct &)

Step R to right (ct 3), stamp on L heel next to R (ct 4)

7-8   Repeat meas 5-6

ORDER OF STEPS

1. First Step: 1x, Second Step: 1x
2. First Step: 1x, Second Step: 1x
3. First Step: 1x, Second Step: 1x
4. First Step: 1x, Second Step: 1x
5. First Step: 1x, Second Step: 1x
6. First Step: 1x, Second Step: 1x

SCOTT'S RAG (USA)

Choreography: By Jim Gold in Ragtime/American folk dance style
Music: Scott Joplin
Formation: Open circle, hands free
Meter: 4/4
Jim Gold YouTube video: *https://www.youtube.com/watch?v=9AJS26DDoIg*
Introduction: 10 measures
Measures:

FIRST STEP
Ragtime Csardas

1 Step R to the right (ct 1), close L to R (ct 2)
  step R to the right (ct 3), touch L next to R (ct 4)

2 Repeat meas 1 opp ft and opp dir
  Suzie Q to the right, CCW

3 Begin with feet together. Then:
  1. Spread feet in opp dir, heels touch (ct 1)
  2. Place weight on L heel and R toes, twist L toes diag right and
  Twist R heel diag right, toes touching (ct 2)
  3. Place weight on L toes and R heel, twist L heel to left,
  Twist R toes to right, heels touch (ct 3)
  4. Place weight on L heel and R toes;
  Twist L toes diag to right, twist R heel to left, heels touch (ct 4)

4 Repeat meas 3
  2 Charleston Steps

5 Step on R (ct 1-2), kick L (ct 3-4)
  Step on L next to R (ct 1-2)
  Touch R far behind L (ct 3-4)

6 Repeat meas 5

7-12 Repeat entire First Step
  On meas 5 (cts 3-4) short hold on R ft

SECOND STEP
8-step cherkessia

1 Cross R over L (ct 1), step on L in place (ct 2)
  Step on R to side of L (ct 3), step on L (ct 4)

2 Repeat meas 1
  8-step grapevine to left, CW

3 Cross R over L (ct 1), step L to side of R (ct 2)

Step R behind L (ct 3), step L to side of R (ct 4)

4   Repeat meas 3

2 Charleston steps: Repeat meas 5-6 from First Step

5-8   Repeat meas 1-4

9-12   Repeat meas 1-4

13-14 Charleston: Repeat meas 5 from First Step

Turn right in full CCW circle: 4 steps

15   R (ct 1-2), L (ct 3-4)

16   R (ct 1-2), L (ct 3-4)

THIRD STEP

Happy Walk: Moving CCW

1   Touch R heel forward, arms move to the right (ct 1)

Step on R ft in place (ct 2)

Touch L heel fwd, arms move to the left (ct 3)

Step on L ft in place (ct 4)

2-8   Repeat meas 1 7x

FOURTH STEP

Simian gallop: Swing arms low

1   Fall on R ft (ct 1)

Step on L about 4 inches from R, arms down and moving back (ct 2)

Fall on R ft (ct 3)

Step on L about 4 inches from R, arms down and moving forward (ct 4)

2-4   Repeat meas 1 3x

5-8   Repeat meas 1-4 turn to right in a full CW circle.

ORDER OF STEPS

1. First Step: 1x, Second Step: 1x, Third Step: 1x, Fourth Step: 1x

2. First Step:

    Break: During slow music:

        Touch R forward (ct 1-2)

        touch R toe to side (ct 3-4)

        Circle R ft (ronde de jambe) (ct 1-2-3)

        Touch R toe to floor (ct 4)

3. Second Step: 1x, Third Step: 1x, Fourth Step: 1x

4. 1. First Step: 1x, Second Step: 1x, Third Step: 1x, Fourth Step: 1x

5. 1. First Step: 1x, Second Step: 1x

SEDNACH DA VETCHERAM (BULGARIA)

Dance Meaning: I sat (down) to dine
Pronunciation: SEDnak da vetCHERiam
Choreography: by Jim Gold in Bulgarian folk dance style
Music: Unknown
Formation: Open circle, arms in W position
Meter: 4/4
Jim Gold Youtube video: *https://www.youtube.com/watch?v=7M3v6EvAToQ*
Introduction: 4 meas: then Second Step 2x
Measures:

FIRST STEP
    Moving LOD: 4 crosses, 2 lifts
    Face fwd

1   Step R to rt (ct 1), cross L over R (ct 2), step R to rt (ct 3), cross L over R (ct 4)

2   Step R to rt (ct 1), lift L (ct 2), step L in place (ct 3), lift R (ct 4)
    Back, fwd

3   Step back on R (ct 1), step L next to R (ct 2), step back on R (ct 3), lft L (ct 4)

4   Step fwd on L (ct 1), close R to L (ct 2)
    Step fwd on L (ct 3), lft L behind R calve(ct 4)

5-8   Repeat meas 1-4

SECOND STEP
    Moving LOD: two 2-steps

1   Step R in LOD (ct 1), step L next to R (ct 2), step R fwd (ct 3-4)

2   Step L in LOD (ct 1), step R next to L (ct 2), step L fwd (ct 3-4)
    8-step grapevine LOD: Face front

3   Step R to rt (ct 1), L behind R with slight dip (ct 2)
    R to rt (ct 3), cross L front of R (ct 4)

4   Repeat meas 3
    Fwd and bck

5   **Fwd into ctr:** R (ct 1), L (ct 2), R (ct 3-4)

6   **Back from ctr:** L (ct 1), R (ct 2), L (ct 3-4)
    Moving RLOD: 4-step grapevine, crossing step

7   Cross R over L with slight dip (ct 1), L next to R (ct 2)
    R behind L with slight dip (ct 3), step L next to R (ct 4)

8   Cross R over L, bringing hands down (ct 1), step L in place (ct 2)

Step R next to L, bring hands up (ct 3-4)

9-12   Repeat meas 5-8

13-14 Repeat meas 1-2

Repeat 8-step grapevine (optional: hand movements down and up

15   Same ft movement as meas 3

(Optional: Hands move down (ct 1-2), hands move up (ct 3-4)

16   Repeat meas 15, arms remain in W position.

17-20 Repeat meas 5-8

ORDER OF STEPS

1. First Step: 1x Second Step: 3x

2. First Step: 1x Second Step: 3x

3. First Step: 1x

SENDERO TRISTE (Cuba)

Dance Meaning: Sad Path
Pronunciation: Sendero Trist e
Choreography: Jim Gold in Cubano-Salsa style
Music: Grupo Polo Montanez from Cuba
Formation: Line dance formation, hands free
Meter: 2/4
Youtube link: *http://bit.ly/2kUmLbj*
Introduction: 10 meas (or Fourth Step)
Measures:

FIRST STEP

Box step

1	Fwd on R (ct 1), L next to R (ct &), R (ct 2)
2	L to lft (ct 1), R next to L (ct &), L (ct 2)
3	Back on R (ct 1), back on L (ct 2)
4	R to rt (ct 1), L next to R (ct &), R (ct 2)
5-8	Repeat meas 1-4 opp ft opp dir

Walks, two-steps, crossing step, turn CW

9	Walk R (ct 1), L (ct 2)
10	R (ct 1), L (ct &), R (ct 2)
11	Walk L (ct 1), R (ct 2)
12	L (ct 1), R (ct &), L (ct 2)

Crossing step and turn

13	Cross R over L (ct 1), step L in place (ct &) Step R next to L (ct 2)
14	Repeat meas 13 opp ft opp dir

Turn left in two steps

15	R (ct 1), L (ct 2)
16	Cross R over L (ct 1), step L in place (ct &) Tch R next to L, no weight (ct 2)
17-32	Repeat meas 1-18

SECOND STEP

Into ctr

1	Step fwd on R (ct 1),step L in place (ct &) Step in place on R (ct 2)
2	Repeat meas 1 back opp ft opp dir
3-4	Repeat meas 1-2

5-6	8-step grapevine CW RLRL RLRL step
	fwd and back lift
7	Step fwd on R (ct 1), lift (or step L (ct 2)
8	Step back on R (ct 1), lft (or step) R(ct 2)
9-14	Repeat meas1-6 of Third Step
	Crossing steps
15	Cross R over L (ct 1), step L in place (ct &)
	Step R next to L (ct 2)
16	Repeat meas 15 opp ft opp dir

THIRD STEP

10 Sides

1-2	Step R to rt (ct 1), close L to rt (ct 2) (a la Mambo step)
3-10	Repeat meas 1 4x

ORDER OF STEPS

1. First Step: 2x
2. Second Step: 2x, Third Step: 1x
3. First Step: 2x, Third Step: 1x
4. First Step: 2x
5. Second Step: 2x
6. First Step: 1x, Third Step: 1x

SHADY GROVE (USA)

Choreography: Jim Gold
Music: Unknown
Formation: Open circle
Meter: 2/4
Jim Gold YouTube teaching video: *https://www.youtube.com/watch?v=vJxtTN-n0d8*
Jim Gold YouTube video: *https://www.youtube.com/watch?v=DPWoH5e079Y*
Introduction: 4 meas

INTRO
Moving CCW

1	Step fwd on R (ct 1), step fwd on L (ct 2)
2	Step fwd on R (ct 1), step on L toe next to R (ct &), step fwd on R (ct 2)
3-4	Repeat meas 1-2 opp ft
5-6	Repeat meas 1-2

4-step grapevine

7	Step L over R (ct 1), step R to rt (ct 2)
8	Step on L behind R (ct 1), close R to L (ct 2)
9	Pause: step on L (ct 1), place R next to L (ct 2)

FIRST STEP
Moving CCW. Long strides,

1	Step fwd on R (ct 1), step fwd on L (ct 2)
2	Step fwd on R (ct 1), step on L toe next to R (ct &) Step fwd on R (ct 2)
3-4	Repeat meas 1-2 opp ft
5-6	Repeat meas 1-2
7	**3-step grapevine** L over R (ct 1), R to rt side (ct 2)
8	Face fwd: step L behind R (ct 1), close R to L (ct 2)

SECOND STEP
Moving into ctr of circle

1	Step fwd on R (ct 1), step fwd on L (ct 2)
2	Step fwd on R (ct 1), step on L toe next to R (ct &) Step fwd on R (ct 2)
3-4	Repeat meas 1-2 opp ft
5-6	Repeat meas 1-2

Back out of circle

7   Step back on L (ct 1), back on R (ct 2)

8   Step L in place (ct 1), step R next to L (ct &), cross L over R (ct 2)

4-step grapevine

9   Step R to rt (ct 1), step L behind R (ct 2)

10   Step R to rt (ct 1), cross L over R (ct 2)

Face CCW

11   Step on R (ct 1), tch L toe next to R (ct 2), press full weight on L (ct &)

ORDER OF STEPS

1. First Step 1x, Second step: 1X
2. First Step 1x, Second step: 1X
3. First Step 1x, Second step: 1X
4. First Step 1x, Second step: 1X: Two grapevines at end, no mea 9
5. First Step 1x, Second step: 1X
6. First Step 1x, Second step: 1X: 3 grapevines at end
7. First Step 1x, Second step: 1X: No meas 9
8. First Step 1x, Second step: 1X: 2 grapevines , place L fwd and hold

SIRBA DE LA VADOUL LOUI ISAK (ROMANIA)

Dance Meaning: Loui Isak's Sirba from Vadoul
Pronunciation: Sirba de la Vadoul Loui Isak
Choreography: by Jim Gold in Romanian folk dance style
Music: Joc Ensemble
Formation: Open Circle, arms in V position
Meter: 4/4
Jim Gold YouTube video: *https://www.youtube.com/watch?v=aDFZ06Lht00*
Introduction: 5 measures
Measures:

FIRST STEP
Sevens right and left
1   Step to R (ct 1), step L behind R (ct &)
2   Step to R (ct 2), step L behind R (ct &)
3   Step to R (ct 3), step L behind R (ct &)
4   Step to R (ct 4), stamp on L next to R no weight (ct &)
5-8   Repeat meas 1-4 opp dir, opp ft.
9-16   Repeat meas 1-8

SECOND STEP
Into ctr and back
1   Step into ctr on R (ct 1), L (ct 2), R (ct 3), hop on R (ct 4)
2   Step bck on L (ct 1), R (ct 2), L (ct 3), hop on L (ct 4)
Grapevine left
3   Step R in front of L (ct 1), step L to side of R (ct 2)
      Step R behind L (ct 3), step L to side of R (ct 4)
4   Repeat meas 3
5-8   Repeat meas 1-4

THIRD STEP
Transition: Lifts and crossing step
Facing ctr
1   Step on R in place (ct 1), lift L (ct 2)
      Step on L in place (ct 3), lift R (ct 4)
2   Repeat meas 1
Crossing step
3   Cross R over L (ct 1), step on L in place (ct 2)
      Step on R in place (ct 3), cross L over R (ct 4)
4   Step on R in place (ct 1), step on L in place (ct 2)
      Cross R in front of L (ct 3), step on L in place (ct 4)
5-6   Repeat meas 1-2
Jump and hold step

7	Cross R over L (ct 1), step on L in place (ct 2)
8	Jump on both feet spread apart and hold 4 cts (ct 3-4, ct 1-2)
	Jump on both feet (ct 3), bring both feet together (ct 4)

Dance Tag: End of Dance Step:
Into ctr and back

1	Step into ctr on R (ct 1), L(ct 2), R (ct 3), hop on R (ct 4)
	Step bck on L (ct 1), step on R in place (ct 2)
2	Step on L (ct 3-4)

ORDER OF STEPS

1. First Step: 1x, Second Step: 1x, Third Step: 1x
2. First Step: 1x, Second Step: 1x
   Four Lifts: (Meas 1-2 of Third Step)
3. First Step: 1x, Second Step: 1x, Third Step: 1x
4. First Step: 1x, Second Step: 1x,
   Four Lifts: (Meas 1-2 of Third Step)
5. First Step: 1x, Second Step: 1x, Third Step: 1x
6. First Step: 1x
   Dance tag: Ending

STANI KUME, STANI (BULGARIA)

Dance Meaning: Stand up, best man (at the wedding)
Pronunciation: Stani, kume, stani
Choreography: by Jim Gold in Bulgarian folk dance style.
Music: Artist unknown. From Veliko Turnovo/Arbanassi. From Jim Gold Tour of
    Bulgaria, 2005.
Formation: Open Circle, arms in V position. Arms swing back on ct 1, fwd on ct 2,
    back on ct 3, fwd on ct 4
Meter: 4/4
Jim Gold YouTube video: *https://www.youtube.com/watch?v=4B18oCJAQHk*
Introduction: 8 measures
Measures:

FIRST STEP
    Moving to the right, arms swing
    Face right
1   Step R, arms swing back (ct 1)
    Step L, arms swing fwd (ct 2)
    Step R to right, arms swing back (ct 3), close L to R, arms swing fwd
(ct 4)
    Moving to the left
2   Step to left on L, arms swing back (ct 1)
    Close R to L, arms swing fwd (ct 2)
    Step to left on L, arms swing back (ct 3)
    Close R to L, arms swing fwd (ct 4)
3-8   Repeat meas 1-2 3x

SECOND STEP
1   Step R (ct 1), step L (ct 2)
    Step R to right (ct 3), close L to R (ct 4)
    Moving to the left: Three push-steps:
2   Fall on L while pushing R ft to side (ct 1), push R (ct 2), push R
    (ct 3)
    Step on R next to L (ct 4), step on L in place (ct &)
3-8   Repeat meas,1-2, 3x

THIRD STEP
    2 Step-hops
1   Step on R (ct 1), hop on R (ct &), step on L (ct 2) hop on L (ct &)
    Face ctr: **3 Crossing:**
2   Step on R (ct 3), cross L in front of R (ct &)
    Step on R in place (ct 4), hop on R (ct &)
    7-Crossing

3   Step on L (ct 1), cross R in front of L (ct &)
         Step on L in place(ct 2), step on R next to L (ct &)
         Step on L in place (ct 3), cross R in front of L (ct &)
         Step on L in place (ct 4), hop on L (ct &)
3-8   Repeat meas 1-2, 3x

STARI ZUPSKI PLES (CROATIA)

Dance Meaning: Dance from the old region
Pronunciation: STA-ri DJUP-ski ("dj"as in leisure) Ples
Choreography: By Jim Gold using traditional steps from Croatia
Source: Dubrovnik Region
Music: Folklorni Ansembl Lindjo: Homo U Kolo
Formation: Circle, arms in V position.
Meter: 4/4
Jim Gold YouTube video: *https://www.youtube.com/watch?v=WibxngggaTI*
Introduction: Wait two measures
Measures:

STEP ONE
(Dance only measures 3-4 for introduction)
Facing left, right shoulder toward ctr

1   Step R into ctr (ct 1), bring L next to R (ct &), step R in ctr (ct 2)
     Back out: Step L out of ctr (ct 3), bring R next to L (ct 4)
2   Repeat meas 1 x
3-4 Repeat meas 1-2

STEP TWO
Sides
Facing ctr, side-together moving right, CCW

1   Step to the right (ct 1), bring L next to R (ct &)
     Step to right (ct 2), bring L next to R (ct &)
     Step to right (ct 3), bring L next to R (ct &)
     Step to the right (ct 4), touch L next to R on inner calve (ct &)
2   Repeat meas 5 in opp ft. opp dir
3-4 Repeat meas 1-2
5-8 Repeat meas 1-4

STEP ONE
Facing left, right shoulder toward ctr

1   Step R into ctr (ct 1), bring L next to R (ct &), step R in ctr (ct 2)
     Back out: Step L out of ctr (ct 3), bring R next to L (ct 4)
2-4 Repeat meas 1 3x

STEP THREE
Sides and cherkessial
1-2 Repeat measures 1-2 of STEP TWO
     Repeat meas 2 in opp ft. opp dir
3   **Cherkessia Step:**
     Cross R over L (ct 1), step on L in place (ct &), step on R to side of

L (ct 2)

Step on L in place (ct &), cross R over L (ct 3)

Step on L in place (ct &), step on R (ct 4)

4   Repeat meas three opp ft

STEP FOUR: (Slow music)

     Rida Step

1   Step R front of L (ct 1), step L to lft side (ct 2)

           R front of L (ct 3), L to left side (ct 4)

2   Step R in front of L (ct 1), step L to lft side (ct 2)

           R in front of L (ct 3), L to left side (ct 4)

3   Step R in front of L (ct 1), step L to lft side (ct 2)

           R in front of L (ct 3), L to left side (ct 4)

4   Step R in front of L (ct 1), step L to left side (ct 2)

           step R in front of L (ct 3), lift L (ct 4)

5-8   Repeat meas 5-8 opp ft, opp dir

     Lame Duck Step

     Facing right, in LOD

1   Hop on L, lifting R in front of L (ct 1), step on R (ct &), step on L (ct 2), hop on L, lifting R in front of L (ct 3), step on R (ct &), step on L (ct 4)

2   Hop on L lifting R in front of L (ct 1), step on R (ct &), step on L (ct 2), hop on L as you half-turn to face CW (ct 3), step on R (ct &), step on L (ct 4)

3-4   Repeat meas 1-2 opp dir and opp ft

     Slow Crossing Cherkessia Step

5   Face ctr: Cross R over L (ct 1), step on L in place (ct 2)

           Step on R to side of L (ct 3), step on L in place (ct 4)

6   Cross R over L (ct 1), step on L in place (ct 2), step on R in place (ct 3)

           step on L in place (ct &), step on R in place (ct 4)

7   Repeat meas 5 opp ft

8   Cross L over R (ct 1), step on R in place (ct 2), step on L in place (ct 3-4)

ORDER OF STEPS

1. First Step 1x, 2 Second Step 1x, First Step 1x, Third Step:1x, Fourth Step 1x

2. First Step 1x, 2 Second Step 1x, First Step 1x, Third Step,1x

3. First Step 1x, 2 Three Step 1x, First Step 1x, Third Step:1x, Fourth Step 1x

4. First Step 1x, 2 Second Step 1x, First Step 1x, Third Step:1x

5. First Step 1x,, Third Step 1x,

     Ending:

1   Step R into ctr (ct 1), bring L next to R (ct &), step R in ctr (ct 2),

           Back out: Step L out of ctr (ct 3), bring R next to L (ct 4),

2   Face fwd: Step on R (ct 1), step L (ct 2), step R (ct 3-4)

STO MI E MILO (BULGARIA)

Dance Meaning: What is Sweet?
Pronunciation: Le-le, VA-rai (Sto Mi E MI-lo)
Choreography: By Jim Gold in Macedonian-Bulgarian folk dance style
Source: Plovdiv Region, Batouchko Monastery area, Lesnoto style
Music: Vievska Folk Group
Formation: Open circle, arms in W position
Meter: 7/8: slow/quick/quick: s, q, q
Jim Gold YouTube video: *https://www.youtube.com/watch?v=tou0AnouAfg*
Introduction: 8 measures
Measures:

FIRST STEP
Lesnoto Step

1	Step to the right on R (s), lift L across R (q), step on L across R (q)
2	Step to the right on R (s), lift L (q, q)
3	Step on L (s), lift R (q, q)

SECOND STEP
Patrioti Step

1-4	Step into ctr with R ft, place L ft behind R knee (s, q, q)
	Step back on L, lift R leg high (s, q, q)
	Hook R ft around in reel step and lock behind L knee (s, q, q)
	Step on R in place (s), place L beside R (q, q)
5	**3 back pas de bas**
	Step on L in place (s), step on R behind (q), step on L in place (q)
6	Repeat meas 5 wi opp dir and opp ft
7	Repeat meas 5 (same dir and ft)
8	Step on R (s), step on L next to R (q, q)

THIRD STEP
Four two-steps to the right, CCW

1	Step forward on R (s), step forward on L (q), step forward on R (q)
2-4	Repeat meas 1 3x
	Three-step grapevine to left, CW
5	R over left (s), L besides R (q), R behind L (q)
	Crossing step
6	Step on L in place (s), cross R in front of L (q), step on L in place (q)
7	Repeat meas 6 opp ft and opp dir
8	Step on L (s), touch R toe to L instep (q, q)

TARGOVSKOTO (BULGARIA)

Dance Meaning: The Merchant. (Fom town of Targovishte in NE Bulgaria)
Pronunciation: Tar GOF skoto
Choreography: by Jim Gold in North Bulgarian folk dance style
Music: Folklore Dances from the Region of Veliko Turnovo
Formation: Line, hands in V or W formation
Meter: 2/4
Jim Gold YouTube video: *https://www.youtube.com/watch?v=Rm5o-r7Q8sI*
Introduction: 8 measures (Leader lifts arms on 7-8)
Measures:

FIRST STEP
Into ctr with 2 two-steps, arms in W position

1   R (ct 1), L (ct &), R (ct 2)
2   L (ct 1), R (ct &), L (ct 2)
3   Step fwd on R (ct 1), kick L fwd (ct 2)
4   Hop back on R (ct 1), step on L (ct &), step on R next to L (ct 2)
5   Step back on L (ct 1), step R next to L (ct &), step on L (ct 2)
      Pas de bas_
6   Step on R (ct 1), cross L over R (ct &), step on R in place (ct 2)
      Slow pas de bas and stamp
7   Step on L next to R (ct 1), cross R over L (ct 2)
8   Step on L in place (ct 1), stamp on R with ft facing diag lft (ct 2)
9-24   Repeat meas 1-8 2x
25-31   Repeat meas 1-7
2   Face ctr: Step on L (ct 1), light stamp on R (ct 2)

SECOND STEP
"Sitno": small, tight, low to the ground steps, moving to rt (LOD)
arms in V position.
      2 "back" two-steps
1   Step fwd on R (ct 1), bring L next to R (ct &), step fwd on R (ct 2)
2   Step fwd on L (ct 1), bring R next to L (ct &), step fwd on L (ct 2)
      Moving to rt (LOD): 2 Step-stamps. and 4 sides
3   Step on R (ct 1), stamp L (ct &), step on L (ct 2), stamp on R (ct 2)
4   Face ctr, leap onto R (ct 1), step L behind R (ct &)
      Step to R toe (ct 2), step L behind R (ct &)
      2 lifts and step behind
5   Step on R (ct 1), lift L (ct 2)
6   Step on L (ct 1), big lift R (ct 2)
7   Cross R in front of L (ct 1), step L next to R (ct 2)
8   Step R behind L (ct 2), step L next to R and face CW (ct 2)

THIRD STEP: (Faster part)
     Into ctr with 2 two-steps. Hands in V position

1   R (ct 1), L (ct &), R (ct 2)

2   L (ct 1), R (ct &), L (ct 2)

3   Step fwd on R (ct 1), kick L fwd (ct 2)

4   Hop back on R (ct 1), step on L (ct &), step on R next to L (ct 2)

5   Step back on L (ct 1), step R next to L (ct &), step on L (ct 2)

    12 crossing steps

6   Step on R (ct 1), cross L over R (ct &)
    step on R in place (ct 2), step L next to R (ct &)

7   Cross R over L (ct 1), step on L in place (ct &)
    Step on R next to L (ct 2), cross L over R (ct &)

8   Step on R in place (ct 1), step on L next to R (ct &)
    Cross R over L (ct 2), step on L in place (&)

9-16   Repeat meas 1-8

ORDER OF STEPS
1. First Step: 4x, Second Step: 3x
1. First step: 2x, Second step: 2x
1. First Step: 4x Second step: 3x
1. First Step: 2x, Second step: 2x

TAYA VETCHER (Bulgaria)

Dance Meaning: This Evening
Pronunciation: Tayah Vetcher
Choreography: by Jim Gold in Bulgarian folk dance style
Music: Unknown
Formation: Line dance, hands in V position
Meter: 9/8. qqqs (quick (2), quick (2), quick(2), slow (3)
Jim Gold YouTube video: *https://www.youtube.com/watch?v=i6myhwX2DVE*
Introduction: 8 measures
Measures:

FIRST STEP
Basic step
Moving CCW: Facing ctr
1   Step R to rt (q), step L behind R (q)
      Step R to rt (1/2q), hop on R, turn to face CCW(1/2q), step on L (s)
Walk 3 steps and point
2   Step fwd on R (q), fwd on L (q), fwd on R (q), point L fwd (s)
Facing CCW: move backwards 3 steps
3   Step bck on L (q), back on R (q), back on L (q), tch R next to L (s)
4-15   Repeat meas 1-3 4x
Break: Face ctr
15   Step R to rt (q), bring L next to R (q)
      step R to rt (q), bring L next to R (s)

SECOND STEP
Into ctr
1   R (q), L (q), R (q), L (s)
2   R (q), L (q), R (q), L (s)
3   Hop on L (q), slap R fwd (q), hop on L (q), slap R diag rt (s)
3 reels back
4   Hop on L (q), step on R behind L (q), hop on R (q), step on L behind R (s)
5   Hop on L (q), step on R behind L (q), step on L next to R (s)
2 cherkasia (crossing) steps
6   Step on R in place (q), cross L over R (q), step on R in place (q) step on L in place (s)
7   Cross R over L (q), step on L in place (q), step on R in place (q) Cross L over R (s)
2 reels
8   Lift R (q), step on R behind L (q), lift L (q), step on L behind R (s)
9   Repeat meas 8
4 stamps

10   Stamp on R close to L (q), stamp on R diag away from L (q)
        Stamp on R close to L (q), stamp on R diag away from L (s)

ORDER OF STEPS
1. First Step: 5x, Second Step: 1x
2. First Step: 5x, Second Step: 1x
3. First Step: 1x, Second Step: 2x
4. First Step: 8x, Second Step: 1x
5. First Step: 5x, Second Step: 2 measures and end

TSHESTATA (BULGARIA)

Dance Meaning: Often, Frequently
Pronunciation: Tshestata
Choreography: by Jim Gold in north Bulgarian folk dance style
Music: Folklore Dances from the Region of Veliko Turnovo
Formation: Open circle, arms down V position
Meter: 7/8 slow/slow/quick/slow (s, s, q. s)
Jim Gold YouTube video: *https://www.youtube.com/watch?v=LSCcIVCjd60*
Introduction: 2 measures "quiet" beats; then 4 more measures
Measures:

FIRST STEP
Hora step: Arms in V position, moving LOD
1   Step R to rt side (s), step on L behind (s)
      Step R to rt side (q), cross L over R (s)
2   Step R to rt side (s), step L behind R(s), step on R(q), lift L (s)
    Move to lft: CW
3   Step L to lft side (s), step R behind (s)
      Step on L (q), lift R (s)

SECOND STEP
Into ctr. Arms in W position
1   R (s), L (s), R (q), hop on R (s)
2   L (s), R (s), L (q), hop (s)
3   R (s), L (s), R (q), hop on R (s)
4   L(s), R (s), L (q), stamp R (s)
    Moving back, out of ctr
5-7   Repeat meas 1-3 going back out of ctr
    Double "twist" stamps
8   L (s), R (s), L (q), turn R leg twds self
      Stamp R diag in twds L (q), stamp R diag out (s)

THIRD STEP
Transition step. Face ctr
Step L to left (s, s), close R to L (q, s)
Step R to rt (s, s), close L to R (q, s)

FOURTH STEP
Arms in W position: Kick, hop
1   Kick R to side (s), hop on L (s)
      Step R behind L (q), step L in place(s)
    5 Rocks
2   Step on R in front of L (q), step back on L (q)

Step on R (q), step on L(q), step on R(q), stamp L heel next to R(s)

3-4   Repeat meas 1-2 opp dir, opp ft
5-8   Repeat meas 1-4
9   Repeat meas 1
10   Leap step onto R to rt side (q), step L behind R (q)

Step R to rt side (q), Step L behind R (q)

Step R to rt side (q)

Stamp L heel next to R (s)

11   Repeat meas 1, opp ft, opp dir
12   Repeat meas, 10 opp ft, opp dir
13-16 Repeat meas 9-12

ORDER OF STEPS

1. First Step: 6 2/3x(20 meas), Second Step: 1x,
    First Step: 8x. Third Step (1x). Fourth Step: 1x
2. First Step: 8x, Second Step: 1x, First Step: 2 2/3x (7 meas), Third Step: 1x,
    Fourth Step: 1x.

THE COSSACKS (Russia)

Choreography: by Jim Gold in Russian folk dance style
Music: Soviet Army Chorus
Formation: Open circle
Style/Mood: Proud
Jim Gold YouTube video: *https://www.youtube.com/watch?v=xB-7f4B1cYE*
Meter 2/4
Introduction: 6 measures

FIRST STEP
Moving LOD, fists on hips
1 Step R (ct 1), L (ct 2)
2 R (ct 1), L (ct &), R (ct 2)
3-4 Repeat meas 1-2 opp ft.
5-8 Repeat meas 1-2 2x

SECOND STEP
Face ctr. Toe-heel.
1 Step R to rt. placing R hand behind head (ct 1), step L behind R (ct 2)
2 Step R to rt (ct 1)
Turn L ft inward, tch L **toe** next to R instep (ct 2)
Turn L ft outward, tch L **heel** next to R instep (ct &)
3-4 Repeat meas 1-2 opp dir
5-8 Repeat meas 1-4

THIRD STEP
Face ctr
Lifts, arms T position, slap, toe-heel
T position, palms facing up
1 Step R to rt (ct1), step L behind R (ct 2)
2 Step R to rt (ct 1), lift L and **slap boot** (ct 2)
3-4 Repeat meas 1-2 opp ft, opp dir
5-6 Repeat meas 1-2
7 Step L to lft (ct 1), cross R behind L (ct 2)
8 Step L to lft, L hand behind head, R fist on rt hip (ct 1),
Turn R ft inward, tch R **toe** next to L instep (ct 2),
Turn R ft outward, tch R **heel** next to L instep (ct &)
9-16 Repeat meas 1-8

ORDER OF STEPS
1. First Step: 1x, Second Step: 1x, Third Step 1x : Arms V position
2. First Step: 1x,, Second Step: 1x, Third Step 1x Arms in V position

3. First Step: (Arms out) 1x, Second Step: 1x, Third Step:1x. (Fist and arms as written above)

4. First Step: 1x (Arms out), Second Step: 1x, Third Step:1x. (Fist and arms as written above)

TIMONYA KRUGOVAYA (RUSSIA)

Dance Meaning: Circle Theme
Pronunciation: Teemonya Krugovaya
Choreographed 1998 Alexandru David. Two additional steps in Russian folk dance
    style added by Jim Gold.
Source: Alexandru David Record
Music: Alexandru David
Formation: Open circle, hands free
Meter: 2/4 (Three measures of 2/4 pattern)
Jim Gold YouTube video: *https://www.youtube.com/watch?v=QWqmnZwrMR0*
Measures:

Introduction: 36 side steps:(Count in 6 measures)
1   Face ctr. Step to rt side with R (ct 1)
       Bring L next to R (ct 2)
2-36 Repeat meas 1 35x (Optional: Alternate meas 1 with:
       Step R to rt side (ct 1-2), bring L next to R (ct 1-2)
       Extended Introduction: (Starts with drum)
1-36 First Step: 6x. **Irregular: 11 measures**
37-46 Second step 10x
47   Face fwd, step R to rt (ct 1)
       Close L next to R (ct 2)

FIRST STEP

Arms back, optional holding hands , 5 moving to rt
1   Bending slightly fwd: Step R to rt with R heel (ct 1), step L behind r
       (ct 2)
2   Repeat meas 1
3   Step R to rt with R heel (ct 1)
       Stand straight as you **jump** on both ft tog (ct 2) bringing hands into
       W position moving to lft. Make sure stamping feet sound rhythm on
       floor.
4   "Fall" on rt ft (ct 1), come up on lft next to R (ct &)
       "Fall" on rt ft (ct 2), come up on lft next to R (ct &)
5   Repeat meas 4
6   Step on R in place (ct 1), step on L in place (ct 2)
7-12 Repeat First Step: Meas 1-6

SECOND STEP

Moving LOD. CWW hands free: "Kursk" Russian two-step
1   While feet dance: Step fwd on R (ct 1), bring L behind R (ct &)
       Step on R in place (ct 2), both hands are up, palms facing dancer
2   Step fwd on L (ct 1), bring R behind L (ct &)
       Step on L in place (ct 2) both hands are up palms facing fwd

3	Repeat meas 1
4	Repeat meas 2
5	Repeat meas 1
6	Repeat meas 2
7-12	Repeat Second Step: Meas 1-6

THIRD STEP

Fists on hips, 3 two-steps into ctr starting with heel

1	Step on R (ct 1), bring L next to R (ct &), step on R (ct 2)
2	Repeat meas 1 opp ft.
3	Repeat meas 1
	3 Reels backj
4	Step back on L (ct 1), lift R in a reel step (ct 2)
5	Repeat meas 4 opp ft
6	Repeat meas 4
	3 pas de bas (or optional 3 syncopated stamp steps)
7	Leap on R next to lft (ct 1), cross L over R (ct &)
	Step on R in place (ct 2)
8	Repeat meas 7 opp ft 2
9	Repeat meas 7
	3 push-steps (optional 5 push-steps on second time)
10	"Fall" on left as you simultaneously push R to rt side (ct 1)
	Step R next to L (ct 2) as you turn head to look at rt boot
11-12	Repeat meas 10 2x (but end with 5 push-steps)
13-24	Repeat Third Step: meas 1-12 (Meas 4-6 arms spreading)

Optional:

13-22	Repeat meas 1-9 of Third Step
	5 push-steps
22	"Fall" on left as you simultaneously push R to rt side (ct 1)
	Step R next to L (ct &)
	"Fall" on left as you simultaneously push R to rt side (ct 2)
	Step R next to L (ct &)
23	Repeat meas 10
24	Step on L (ct 1), place R next to L (ct 2)

FOURTH STEP

5 "Big Moving" Steps CWW
Fists remain on hips

1	Big step R to rt with R heel (ct 1), step L behind R (ct 2)
2	Repeat meas 1
3	Step R to rt with R heel (ct 1), small kick L ft (with square heel in front or R
	Moving into ctr, fists on hips, lft shlder leans into ctr
4	Step on L (ct 1), bring R behind L (ct 2)

5	Repeat meas 4
6	Step on L (ct 1), step (optional: stamp) R behind L (ct 2) **"Falling backwards" out of circle. Simultaneously place R hand behind head (nape of neck), place L fist on L hip**
7	"Fall" on L behind R, simultaneously lift R leg, face fwd (ct 1) Step on R next to L (ct 2)
8	Repeat meas 7
9	Step on R (ct 1), tch L next to R no wt (ct 2) **Three push-steps. Place R fist on R hip. Look at rt boot**
10	"Fall" on L as you simultaneously push R to rt side (ct 1) Step R next to L(2)
11	**Double push-step:** "Fall" on L as you simultaneously push R to rt side (ct 1) Step R next to L (ct &) "Fall" on left as you simultaneously push R to rt side (ct 2) Step R next to L (ct &)
12	Step on L (ct 1), step on R next to L (ct 2)
13-24	Repeat Fourth Step: meas 1-12

ORDER OF STEPS
Introduction: Side steps 26 meas
Extended Introduction: First Step: 6x, Second Step: 2x

Dance starts with singing sound of "Yes"
1.   Step I: 2x
           Step II: 2x
           Step III: 1x
           Step IV: 1x

2.   Step I: 2x
           Step II: 2x
           Step III: 2x
           Step IV: 2x
           Repeat pattern 2 until end.
           Ends with Third Step

TISH KAZALA (UKRAINE)

Dance Meaning: You Said
Pronunciation: Tish Ka-ZA-la
Choreography: By Jim Gold using traditional steps from Ukraine.
Source: Typical Ukranian steps.
Music: Burya III: Ron Cahute and Burya
Formation: Open circle: Hands on hips
Meter: 4/4
Jim Gold Youtube video: *https://www.youtube.com/watch?v=AUc-7DJQHco&t=62s*
Introduction: 8 measures
Measures:

PART ONE

FIRST STEP
    Running Step, hands on hips
    Moving to the right, CCW, run 4 steps, kick legs back
1   R (ct 1), L (ct 2), R (ct 3), L (ct 4)
2   Step on R (ct 1), hop on R (ct 2)
    Step on L (ct 3), hop on L (ct 4)
3-12   Repeat meas 1-2 five more times

SECOND STEP
    In and out of ctr
    Face ctr, lead with R heel 4 Russian two-steps
1   Step into ctr on R (ct 1), bring L behind R heel (ct &)
    Step slightly forward on R (ct 2), step forward on L (ct 3)
    Bring R behind L heel (ct &), step slightly forward on L (ct 4)
2   Repeat meas 1
    8 Reels bkwds
3   Lift R, place behind L (ct 1)
    Lift L, place behind R (ct 2)
    Lift R, place behind L (ct 3)
    Lift L, place behind R (ct 4)
4   Repeat meas 3
5-12 Repeat meas 1-4 2x

THIRD STEP
    Toe-heel
    Face ctr: Put left hand behind head (cradling medulla region) Russian style
1   Touch R toe to right while bending R knee towards L knee (ct 1)

Twist R ft out, touch R heel in same spot (ct 2)
Step on R in place (ct 3), step on L in place (ct &)
Step on R in place (ct 4)

2   Repeat meas 1 using opp hand and opp ft

3-8   Repeat meas 1-2 3x

FOURTH STEP

4 front pas de bas steps

1   Step on R in place (ct 1), cross L in front of R (ct &)
Step on R in place (ct 2)
Step on L in place (ct 3), cross R in front of L (ct &)
Step on R in place (ct 4)

2   Repeat meas 1 3x

2 syncopated steps in place:

Step on R (ct 1), tap L heel next to R (ct &)
Lift L ft (ct 2), tap L next to R (ct &)
Step on L (ct 3), tap R heel next to L (ct &)
Lift R ft (ct 4), tap R next to L (ct &)

4 heel-brush steps into ctr

4   Step forward on R (ct 1), brush L heel (ct &)
Step forward on L (ct 2), brush R heel (ct &)
Step forward on R (ct 3), brush L heel (ct &)
Step forward on L (ct 4), brush R heel (ct &)

5-7   Repeat meas 1-3

8   Repeat meas 3 of Second Step: (4 Reels back)

FIFTH STEP

Toe-heel-lift-push step
Face ctr: Put left hand behind head (cradling medulla region)
Russian style

1   Touch R toe to right while bending right knee towards left knee (ct 1)
Twist R ft out, touch R heel in same spot (ct 2)
Touch sole of R ft to inner calf of L leg (ct 3)
Push R ft to the right (ct 4)

2   Fall on R ft while turning L leg out to left (ct 1)
twist L ft out, touch L heel in same spot (ct 2)
Touch sole of L ft to inner calf of L leg (ct 3)
Push L ft to left (ct 4)

3-7   Repeat meas 1-2 3x

8   Fall on R ft while turning L leg out to left (ct 1)
Twist L ft out, touch L heel in same spot (ct 2)
Step on L next to R (ct 3)
Step on R next to L (ct &)
Step on L in place (ct 4)

SIXTH STEP

In place and sides

1   Step on R (ct 1), step on L (ct &)
     Step on R, push left leg to left side (ct 2)
     Step on L (ct 3), step on R (ct &)
     Step on L, push R leg to right side (4)
2-4 Repeat meas 1 3x

SEVENTH STEP

Slaps and claps
Standing with weight on L ft

1   Slap L side of hip with L hand (ct 1)
     Raise R leg and slap above R knee (ct &)
     Step on R (ct 2)
     Clap both hands (ct 3)
     Jump on both ft (ct 4)
2   Clap both hands in front of chest (ct 1)
     Slap L thigh with R hand (ct &)
     Clap both hand in front of chest (ct 2)
     Slap R thigh with L hand (ct &)
     Slap R thigh with R hand (ct 3)
     Slap L thigh with L hand (ct &)
     Clap both hands in front of chest (ct 4)
3   Step on L (ct 1)
     Raise R leg and slap R quadriceps above knee (ct 2)
     Step on R (ct 3)
     Raise L leg and slap L quadriceps above knee (ct 4)
4   Clap both hands(1-2), slap R thigh (3-4)
5-7 Repeat meas 1-3
8   Clap both hands, step on L (ct 1-2)
     Bend forward, slap R boot with R hand, L arm moves diag upwards
     to left (ct 3-4)

PART TWO

Repeat entire above sequence.

TO DILINO (TO ΔΕΙΛΙΝΟ) (Greece)

Meaning το δελινόι: Sunset
Pronunciation: Dee lee no
Choreography: Jim Gold in Greek folk dance style
Music: Constantin Paravanos: Greece (Music Around the World)
Formation: Open circle, hands in W or V position as indicated
Meter: 7/8 counted S/q/q. (S=3, q=2, q=2: Total cts 7) , Third Step: and 7/8 q/q/S
(Note: S can be broken up into 2 and 1. See THIRD STEP)
Style: Springy
Youtube video link: *http://bit.ly/2pjLEzE*
Introduction: 8 measures
Measures:

FIRST STEP

Moving LOD, CCW, facing ctr, hands in W position (Solo leader arms T position)

1   Step R to rt (ct s), step L behind R (ct q), step R to rt (ct q)
2   Cross L over R (ct s), step R next to L (ct q), step L fwd (ct q)
     2 back pas de bas
3   Step R to rt (ct s), step L behind R (ct q), step R in place (ct q)
4   Repeat meas 3 opp dir, opp ft

SECOND STEP

Into ctr and back, solo leaders arms in W position

1   Step R fwd (ct s), step L next to R (ct q), step R fwd (ct q)
2   Repeat meas 1 opp ft
     Back pas de bas
3   Step R to rt (ct s), step L behind R (ct q), step R in place (ct q)
4   Repeat meas 3 opp dir, opp ft
5-6 Repeat meas 1-2 moving back
7   Repeat meas 3
8   Step on L (ct s), **hands move to V position**

THIRD STEP

Meter changes to 8/8, arms V position
7 crossing steps: cherkesia 7, and rest

1   Cross R front of L (ct 1), L in place L (ct 2), back on R (ct 3), L in place (ct 4)
     fwd on R (ct 5), L in place (ct 6), step on R to L (ct 7-8)
     7 sides CW
2   Step L to lft (ct 1), step R behind L (ct 2), step L to lft (ct 3). R behind L (ct 4)
     Step L to lft (ct 5), step R behind L (ct 6), step on L (ct 7-8)

— 201 —

3	Repeat meas 1
4	Repeat meas 2, tch R toe (ct 7-8)
5-8	Repeat meas 1-4
9	Tch R toe next to L (1-2)

ORDER OF STEPS
1. First Step: 2x, Second Step:1x,Third Step: 1x

TOREADOR (France)

Dance Meaning: Bull fighter on horseback
Pronunciation: Tor ay a door
Choreography: Jim Gold in mixed folk style
Music: Toreador Song from Opera Carmen by George Bizet
Formation: Open circle (line dance), no hand hold
Meter: 4/4
Youtube link: *http://bit.ly/2lJEXCt*
Introduction: 8 meas
Measures:

FIRST STEP
Bull charge step! (Index and thumb touching, middle, ring and pinky spread upward.

1-2 Step fwd R (ct 1), step fwd L (ct 2), step fwd R (ct 3), kick L (ct 4)

3-4 Step back on L (ct 1), back on R (ct 2), back on L (ct 3), stamp R (ct 4)

Cloak step: Hands in holding cloak position

5-6 Step R to rt (ct 1), step L behind R (ct 2), step R to rt (ct 3), stamp L(ct 4)

7-8 Step L to lft (ct 1), step R behind L (ct 2), step L to lft (ct 3), stamp on R (ct 4)

9-16 Repeat meas 1-8

SECOND STEP
4 grapevines CW, hands V position

1 Grapevine 8

2 R (ct 1), L (ct 2), R (ct 3), L (ct 4)

3 R (ct 1), L (ct 2), R (ct 3), L (ct 4)

4 R (ct 1), L (ct 2), R (ct 3), L (ct 4)

Ctr and back

5 R (ct 1), L (ct 2), R (ct 3), lift L (ct 4)

6 L (ct 1), R (ct 2), L (ct 3), lift R (ct 4)

7 Stamp and hold R(ct 1-2), stamp and hold R(ct 3-4)

(Repeat FIRST STEP)

Transition:
Cherkesia 8

1 Cross R front of L (ct 1), step L in place (ct 2)
Step R back of L (ct 3), step L in place (ct 4)

2 Repeat meas 1, raising hands, arms parallel to floor, hold cape on right side

THIRD STEP: Cape Step
      4 grapevines, holding cloak

1-4:	**Step R to rt** (ct 1) **4 grapevines**
5	Turn CCW in 4 steps, RLRL

      ctr and back

6	Step R fwd (ct 1), step L fwd (ct 2), step R fwd (ct 3), lift L (ct 4) (Drop cape) Hands move to V position
7	Step back on L (ct 1), step back on R (ct 2), step back on L (ct 3), lift R (ct 4)

      Sway and tap

8	Step on R (ct 1), tap L next to R (ct 2), step on L (ct 3), tap R next to L (ct 4)
9	Sway to rt on R (ct 1), step on L in place (ct 2)

      Three crosses: Cross R over L (ct 3), step L (ct 4)

10	Cross R over L (ct 1), step L (ct 2), cross R over L (ct 3), lift L (ct 4)
11	**Two crosses:** Cross L over R (ct 1), step R (ct 2). Cross L over R (ct 3), step R (ct 4)
12	Cross L over R (ct 1-2), lift R (ct 2). Tch/tap R toe (ct 3-4)
13-23	Repeat meas 1-21 THIRD STEP
24	Cross L over R (ct 1), lift R (ct 2)

TOUT VA TRES BIEN (France)

Dance Meaning: All Goes Very Well
Pronunciation: Too Va Tray Byen
Choreography: by Jim Gold
Music: Le Canard Bleu . Song written by Paul Misraki
Formation: Open circle, arms down in V position
Meter: 4/4
Jim Gold Youtube video: *https://www.youtube.com/watch?v=hpQVL-CBZLs*
Introduction: 10 measures
Measures:

FIRST STEP

4 front pas de bas

1   Step on R (ct 1), cross L front of R (ct &), step R in place (ct 2)
    Step on L (ct 3), cross R front of L (ct &), L in place (ct 4)
2-4   Repeat meas 1 3x

8 cross steps CW (to left) "Horse step"

3   Cross R over L (ct 1), L behind R lift free R leg high: "horse step" (ct 2)
    Cross R over L (ct 3), L behind R (ct 4)
4   Repeat meas 3
5-8   Repeat meas 1-4
9-10   Repeat meas 1-2

Complete **8 step turn** in place to left (on toes)

11   R (ct 1), L (ct 2), R (ct 3), L (ct 4)
12   R (ct 1), L (ct 2), R (ct 3), L (ct 4)
13-16 Repeat meas 1-4

Walk 4 steps fwd

17   R (ct 1-2), L (ct 3-4)
18   R (ct 1-2), L (ct 3-4)

Csardas steps diag back

19   R to rt (ct 1), L tog (ct 2), R to rt (ct 3), tch L next to R (ct 4)
20   L to left (ct 1), R tog (ct 2), L to left (ct 3), tch R next to L (ct 4)

8 step turn rt

Walk stiff-stepped (locked knees) in complete circle to right

21   R (ct 1), L (ct 2), R (ct 3), L (ct 4)
22   R (ct 1), L (ct 2), R (ct 3), L (ct 4)
23-24 Repeat meas 1-2
25   Fwd R (ct1), L (ct 2), R (ct 3-4)
26   Back L (ct 1-2), tch R heel (ct 3-4)

SECOND STEP

Repeat meas 1-18

Ending:

6 Csardas steps diag back

9   R (ct 1), L tog (ct 2), R (ct 3), tch L next to R (ct 4)

10   L (ct 1), R tog (ct 2), L (ct 3), tch R next to L (ct 4)

11-14 Repeat meas 9-10 2x

15-16 **Walk-turn: 8 steps in a circle: CW**

       R (ct 1), L (ct 2), R (ct 3), L (ct 4)

       R (ct 1), L (ct 2), R (ct 3), L (ct 4)

17-18 Repeat meas 1-2

19   Fwd R (ct1), L (ct 2), R (ct 3-4)

20   Back L (ct 1-2), tch R heel (ct 3-4)

Interlude:

21   Step R to rt (ct 1-2), close L to R (ct 3-4)

       Last step: Meas 21 2x

ORDER OF STEPS

1. First Step: 3x
2. First Step with ending: 1x

Ending

2 front pas de bas, 1 fwd pas de bas, step back and toe

1   Step on R (ct 1), cross L front of R (ct &), step R in place (ct 2)

      Step on L (ct 3), cross R front of L (ct &), L in place (ct 4)

2   Step fwd on R (ct 1), step L next to R (ct &), step R in place (ct 2)

      Step back on L (ct 3), draw R toe to L ft (ct 4)

Tout Va Tres Bien

by Paul Misraki

   Paul Misraki, de son vrai nom Paul Misrachi, est un compositeur, auteur, et chanteur français né le 28 janvier 1908 à Constantinople et mort le 29 octobre 1998 à Paris. Compositeur et pianiste de Ray Ventura dans les années 1930, il est aussi un écrivain ayant publié dix livres sur des sujets liés à son itinéraire sprituel.

   Part 1

Allô, allô, James, quelles nouvelles

Absente depuis quinze jours,

Au bout du fil je vous appelle

Que trouverai- je à mon retour ?

Tout va très bien, madame la Marquise
Tout va très bien, tout va très bien
Pourtant il faut, il faut que l'on vous dise
On déplore un tout petit rien
Un incident, une bêtise,
La mort de votre jument grise
Mais à part ça, Madame la Marquise
Tout va très bien, tout va très bien !

Part 2
Allô, allô, Martin, quelles nouvelles
Ma jument grise, morte aujourd'hui ?
Expliquez moi, cocher fidèle,
Comment cela s'est- il produit ?
Cela n'est rien, madame la Marquise
Cela n'est rien, tout va très bien,
Pourtant il faut, il faut que l'on vous dise
On déplore un tout petit rien
Elle a périt dans l'incendie
Qui détruisit vos écuries
Mais à part ça, madame la Marquise
Tout va très bien, tout va très bien !

Part 3
Allô, allô, Pascal, quelles nouvelles
Mes écuries ont donc brûlé ?
Expliquez moi, mon chef modèle
Comment cela s'est- il passé
Cela n'est rien, madame la Marquise,
Cela n'est rien, tout va très bien !
Pourtant il faut, il faut que l'on vous dise
On déplore un tout petit rien
Si l'écurie brûla madame,
C'est qu'le château était en flamme,
Mais à part ça, madame la Marquise
Tout va très bien, tout va très bien !

Part 4
Allô, allô, Lucas, quelles nouvelles
Notre château est donc détruit ?

Expliquez moi car je chancelle !
Comment cela s'est- il produit ?

Eh! bien voilà, madame la Marquise
Apprenant qu'il était ruiné
A peine fut- il rev'nu de sa surprise
Qu' Monsieur l'Marquis s'est suicidé

Et c'est en ramassant la pelle
Qu'il renversa toutes les chandelles
Mettant le feu à tout l'château
Qui s'consuma de bas en haut
Le vent souflant sur l'incendie,
Le propageant sur l'écurie
Et c'est ainsi qu'en un moment
On vit périr votre jument

Mais à part ça, madame la Marquise
Tout va très bien,tout va très bien !

U ŠAPCU KRAJ SAVE (Serbia)

Šabac (Serbian Cyrillic: Шабац,) pronounced Shabatz

Dance Meaning: (I Loved) In Šabac, Next to the Sava (River)
Pronunciation: Oo Shaptsoo Kraee Sava
Choreography: by Jim Gold in Serbian folk dance style
Music: Ljuba Alicic group: *https://www.youtube.com/watch?v=ciuhnWWCck0*
Formation: Open circle
Style and Mood: Proud, happy, joyful, upbeat
Meter: 2/4
Jim Gold Youtube video: *https://bit.ly/2OpGkV1*
Introduction: 8 measures
Measures:

FIRST STEP
Moving step CCW
1   Step diag to rt on R (ct 1), step diag to lft on L (ct 2)
2   Moving fwd: step R (ct 1), step L (ct &), step on R (ct 2)
3   Step diag to lft on L (ct 1), step diag to rt on R (ct 2)
4   Moving fwd: step on L (ct 1), step on R (ct &) step on L (ct 2)
5-8   Repeat meas 1-4

SECOND STEP
Hora step
1   Step R to rt (ct 1), cross L over R (ct 2)
2   Step on R (ct 1), turn slightly lft, look left, feet point diag left, and tch L (ct 2)
3   Step on L (ct 1), turn slightly rt, look right, feet point diag right, and tch R (ct 2)
4-30 Repeat meas 1-3 (9x)

ORDER OF STEPS
1. First Step: 2x, Second Step: 10
2. First Step: 2x, Second Step: 10
3. First Step: 2x, Second Step: 10

Words to Song in Serbian and English

U Šapcu Kraj Save

Voleo sam u Šapcu kraj Save
jednu malu, njene oči plave

Ref. 2x

Jednu malu, njene oči plave
ljubio sam na obali Save

Često mi se u snovima jave
naše duge šetnje pored Save

Ref. 2x

Uvek kad sam u Šapcu kraj Save
ja poželim njene oči plave

I Loved in Sabac, Next to the Sava

I loved in Sabac, next to the Sava
one little one, her blue eyes

Chorus 2x

One little one, her blue eyes
I was kissing on the Sava´s coast

Our long walkings next to the Sava
appears into my dreams often

Chorus 2x

I wish her blue eyes
always when I'm in Sabac, next to the Sava

Chorus 2x

U SEST NUMBER 7 (SERBIA)

Dance Meaning: U sest mean "in Six."
Bob's U Sest: Named after Bob Radcliffe because I got the music from Bob
  or U Sest Number 7
Pronunciation: Oo Shest
Choreography: By Jim Gold using traditional steps from Serbia
Music: Obtained from Bob Radcliffe
Formation: Line
Meter: 2/4
Jim Gold YouTube video: *https://www.youtube.com/watch?v=yKhgBTl-44U*
Introduction: 8 measures
Measures:

FIRST STEP
Basic U Sest Step:
1   Walk to right R (ct 1), L (ct 2)
2   Face ctr: step R (ct 1), touch L next to R (ct 2)
3   Step to left on L (ct 1), touch R next to L (ct 2)
4   Step to right on R (ct 1), touch L next to R (ct 2)
5-8 Repeat in opp dir and opp ft

SECOND STEP
1   Step on R (ct 1), hop on R (ct 2), cross L over R (ct &)
2   Step on R (ct 1), step on L next to R (ct 2), step on R next to L (ct &)
3   Repeat meas 2 using opp ft
4   Repeat meas 2
5-8 Repeat meas 1-4 opp ft and opp dir

THIRD STEP
Two-steps
Moving right, CCW: 3 two-steps
1   R (ct 1), L (ct &), R (ct 2)
2   L (ct 1), R (ct &), L (ct 2)
3   R (ct 1), L (ct &), R (ct 2)
4   Step on L while shouting Op (ct 1)
     Lift R and swing to move in opp dir while
     shouting **sa!** (ct 2) (Complete shout: **Opsa!**)
     7 crossing steps CW, body faces front
5   Cross R over L (ct 1), step on L next to R (ct 2)
6   Repeat meas 5
7   Repeat meas 5
8   Cross R over L (ct 1), lift L (ct 2)
9-16 Repeat meas 1-8 with opp ft and in opp dir

FOURTH STEP

Two-steps Moving right, CCW

1   1 two-step: R (ct 1), L (ct &), R (ct 2)

2   Step on L (ct 1), lift R, swing to left preparing to move in opp dir (ct 2)

7 quick crossing steps CW, body faces front

3   Cross R over L (ct 1), step on L next to R (ct &)
      Cross R over L (ct 1), step on L next to R (ct &)

4   Cross R over L (ct 1), step on L next to R (ct &)
      Step on R (ct 1-2)

5-8   Repeat meas 1-4 in opp dir with opp ft

9   **4 into ctr 2 two-steps into ctr**
      Step fwd on R (ct 1), step L next to R (ct &), step fwd on R (ct 2)

10   Repeat meas 1 using opp ft

11   Facing ctr, step on R (ct 1), tap L next to R as you bend fwd (ct 2)

12   Straighten body, step back on L (ct 1), step R in place (ct 2)

13   Step on L (ct 1), lift R (ct 2)

14   Step on R(ct 1), lift L touching R calf, turn 1/4 to left (ct 2)

7 side-together steps moving diagonally out of circle

15   Step out of circle on L (ct 1), bring R next to L (ct &)
      Step out of circle on L (ct 2), bring R next to L (ct &)

16   Step out of circle on L (ct 1), bring R next to L (ct &), step on L (ct 2)

UNA NOCE AL LUNAR (BOSNIA)

Dance Meaning: One Moonlight Night
Pronunciation: Oona Notche al Loonar: Sung in Ladino.
Choreography: by Jim Gold in Bosnian (Balkan) folk dance style
Music: Flory Jagoda: Memories of Sarajevo
Formation: Open circle, hands V or W position
Meter: 2/4
Jim Gold YouTube video: *https://www.youtube.com/watch?v=1rt1x1fZdsk*
Introduction: 6 measures
Measures:

FIRST STEP: (Starts when voice sings "Una")
    Crossing steps moving right: Hands in V position
1   Step to R (ct 1), cross L over R (ct &)
    step to R (ct 2), cross L over R (ct &)
2   Step R to rt (ct 1), step on L next to R (ct &)
    Cross R over L (ct 2)
    Cross steps, full turn: hands in W position
3   Step on L to lft side (ct 1). Full turn CCW, step on R (ct 2)
4   Step L to left (ct 1), step on R to rt side of L (ct &)
    Cross L over R (ct 2)

SECOND STEP
    Into ctr
    Walk on a straight line into ctr
1   Step fwd on R (ct 1), step fwd on L (ct 2)
    Cherkessia 3, step fwd
2   Cross R over L (ct 1), step on L in place (ct &)
    Step on R next to L (ct 2), step fwd on L (ct&)
3   Tch R toe (ct 1), tch R heel (ct &)
    Moving back, out of ctr
    Lift R (ct 2), step back on R (ct &)
4   Lift L (ct 1), step back on L (ct &)
    Step on R (ct 2), step on L next to R (ct &)
5-8   Repeat meas 1-4 of Third Step
    On meas 4, hands move down to V position.

THIRD STEP
    Transition: 3 Hora Steps. Hands in V position
1   Step to R (ct 1), cross L over R (ct &)
    Step on R next to L (ct 2), tch L next to R (ct &)
2   Step to left of L (ct 1), tch R next to L (ct &)
    Step to R (ct 2), cross L over R (ct &)

3	Step on R next to L (ct 2), tch L next to R (ct &)
	Step to left of L (ct 1), tch R next to L (ct &)
4	Step to R (ct 1), cross L over R (ct &)
	Step on R next to L (ct 2), tch L next to R (ct &)
5	Step on L to side next to R (ct 1)
	Draw rt ft twds L raising hands to W position (ct 1)
	Tch rt toe next to L (ct 2)

ORDER OF STEPS
1. First Step: 1x, Second Step: 2x, Third Step: 1x
2. First Step: 1x, Second Step: 2x, Third Step: 2x
3. First Step: 1x, Second Step: 2x, Third Step: 1x
4. First Step: 1x, Second Step: 2x, Third Step: 1x

VAJZAL E PERMETIT (ALBANIA)

Dance Meaning: Girls of Permetit
Pronunciation: Vajzal e Permetit
Choreography: by Jim Gold in Albanian folk style
Music: Albanian folk music
Formation: Open circle, arms up, W position
Meter: 4/4
Jim Gold YouTube video: *https://www.youtube.com/watch?v=egvoiBLOLQQ*
Introduction: 2 meas Then dance intro step
Measures:

FIRST STEP
Seven Pogonishte steps: fwd, lift
1 Step R to rt (ct 1-2), step L behind R (ct 3), step R to rt (ct 4)
2 Cross L over R (ct 1-2), step R next to L (ct 3), L to lft (ct 4)
3-6 Repeat meas 1-2 2x
7 Step R to rt (ct 1-2), step L behind R (ct 3), step R to rt (ct 4)
8 Step fwd on L (ct 1-2), lift R and hold (ct 3-4)
Touch, Lift, Albanite left, Albanite right
9 Tch R fwd (ct 1-2), tch R diag rt (ct 3-4)
10 Step back on R (ct 1), step L next to R (ct 2)
Step fwd on R next to L (ct 3-4)
11 Tch L fwd (ct 1-2), tch L diag lft (ct 3-4)
12 Step back on L (ct 1), step R next to L (ct 2), step fwd on L next to R (ct 3-4)
8-step grapevine
13 R to rt (ct 1), L behind R (ct 2), R to rt (ct 3), L front of R (ct 4)
14 Repeat meas 9
2 pogonishte steps
15-16 Repeat meas 1-2

SECOND STEP
Move CW, facing front
1 Cross R over L (ct 1-2), step L to lft (ct 3), cross R over L (ct 4)
2 Step L to lft (ct 1-2), cross R in front of L (ct 3-4)
3 Repeat meas 2
Albanite left (Yemenite left)
4 Step on L (ct 1), step R next to L (ct 2), cross L over R (ct 3-4)

ORDER OF STEPS
1. First Step: 1x, Second Step: 1x
Repeat order of steps

VARKA STO YIALO (Greece)

Dance Meaning: Varka Sto Yialo means: Boat on the Beach
Pronunciation: VAR-ka Sto Yial-O
Choreography: By Jim Gold in Greek folk dance style
Music: The Greek Way
Formation: Line. Arms in V position
Meter: 2/4
Jim Gold YouTube video:
   1. Teaching: *https://www.youtube.com/watch?v=bpqI3xXWU98*
   2 Performing: *https://www.youtube.com/watch?v=oGi7Tt59s6I*
Introduction: One measure
Measures:

FIRST STEP
   Moving right, CCW: 2 two-steps
1   R (ct 1)), L (ct &), R (ct 2)
2   Repeat meas 1 with opp ft
   Facing ctr, moving CW, 8 cross steps
3   Cross R over L (ct 1), bring L next to R (ct &)
     Cross R over L (ct 2), bring L next to R (ct &)
4   Repeat meas 3
5-8 Repeat meas 1-4
   Twist-cross
9   Face ctr, cross R over L (ct 1), cross L over R (ct 2)
10   Cross R over L (ct 1), step on L behind R (ct &), step on R slightly to
     left (ct 2)
   Travel out of ctr in 7 steps, left shoulder facing out of circle
11   Step on L (ct 1), bring R next to L (ct &). step on L(ct 2), bring R
     next to L (ct &)
12   Step on L (ct 1), bring R next to L (ct &), step on L (ct 2)
13-16 Repeat meas 9-12

SECOND STEP: HORA STEP
   Moving to right, CCW
1   Step on R (ct 1), cross L over R (ct 2)
2   Step on R (ct 1), touch (or lift) L (ct 2)
3   Step on L (ct 1), touch (or lift) R (ct 2)
4-38 Repeat meas 1-3 12x
     End: step on R in place (ct 1), step on L next to R (ct 2)

VRADIAZI (Greece)

Dance Meaning: Evening Falls
Pronunciation: Vra-DIA-zi
Choreography: By Jim Gold using Greek hasapico (butcher's dance) folk dance
   style
Music: Mikos Theodorakis
Formation: Open circle. Shoulder hold, or arms in W position
Meter: 2/4
Jim Gold Youitube video: *ttps://www.youtube.com/watch?v=k9HChOGh75Y*
Introduction: 4 measures
Measures:

Intro step:
1	Step R to rt (ct 1), close L to R (ct-2)
2	Step L to lft (ct 1), close R to L (ct 2)
3-4	Repeat meas 1-2

FIRST STEP
Basic Hasapico step

1   Heavy fall forward on L (ct 1)
      Touch R toe behind L (ct &)
      Lift R in reel step (ct 2), place R behind L (ct &)

2   Lift L in a reel step (ct 1)
      Place L behind R (ct &)
      Lift R (ct 2)

Walk 2 steps to the right

3   R (ct 1), L (ct &)
      Step back on R (ct 2)

Touch toe twice, "falling forward" step

4   Touch L toe on outside of right ft (ct 1)
      Touch L toe on outside of right ft again (ct 2)

5   Lift L and place L ankle above R knee, hold one count as you lean
      (fall) fwd (ct 1)
      Heavy fall forward on L (ct 2), touch R toe behind L (ct &)

6   Lift R in reel step (ct 1), place R behind L (ct &)
      Lift L in a reel step (ct 2), place L behind R and lift R (ct &)

6-15 Repeat step 3x

SECOND STEP

1   **Moving CW**
      4 crosses
      Cross R over L (ct 1), step on L (ct &), cross R over L (ct 2), step
      on L (ct &)

2   Cross R over L(ct 1), step on L (ct &), step on R (ct 2)
            Swing L around to change directions by crossing L over R (ct &)

3 crosses CWW

3   Cross L over R (ct 1), step on R (ct &), cross L over R (ct 2), step
            on R (ct &)

4   Cross L over R (ct 1), lift R (ct 2)
            Swing L around to change directions (ct &)

Into ctr

5   Step fwd on R (ct 1), step fwd on L (ct 2)

6   Step fwd on R (ct 2) touch L toe behind R (ct &)

Back out of ctr

7   Step back on L (ct 1)
            Step back on R (ct 2), bring L next to R (ct &)

Sides

8   Step diag right back on R (ct 1)
            Close L to R (ct 2)

9   Step L to lft (ct 1), close R to L (ct 2)

ORDER OF STEPS

1. First step: 3x   Second step: 1x
2. First step: 3x   Second step: 1x
3. First step: 3x   Second step: 1x
4. First step: 3x

WILDWOOD FLOWER (USA)

Choreography: Jim Gold in international folk dance style
Music: Sung by Keith Whitley
Formation: Open circle, arms in V position, thumbs behind (holding) belt buckles
Meter: 2/4
Jim Gold Youtubes video: https://www.youtube.com/watch?v=8KJZqNmQ5Sc
Introduction. No introduction, start right away (after up beat).
Measures:

FIRST STEP
Into ctr and back, arms in V position

1   Step R fwd (ct 1), scuff L (ct &), step L fwd (ct 2), scuff R (ct &)
2   Step R fwd (ct 1), scuff L (ct &), tch L fwd (ct 2)
3   Step L back (ct 1), R back (ct 2)
4   L back (ct 1), tch R next to L (ct 2)
5   Step R to rt (ct 1), close L to R (ct 2)
6-10   Repeat meas 1-5

SECOND STEP
**Moving LOD, facing LOD. Thumbs behind (holding) belt buckles
6 step-scuff steps**

1   Step R (ct 1) scuff L (ct &), step L (ct 2), scuff R (ct &)
2-3   Repeat meas 1 2x
4   5 sides: Face ctr: R (ct 1), close L to R (ct 2)
5-9   Repeat meas 4 3x

ORDER OF STEPS
1. First Step: 1x, Second Step: 1x

YA, IZLIAZ, DONKE (Bulgaria)

Dance Meaning: Go Out (Step Out), Donke
Pronunciation: Ya eezleyaz, Donka
Choreography: by Jim Gold in Bulgarian folk dance style
Music: Bulgarian Folk Dances and Songs
Formation: Open circle leads to the right (counter clockwise), hands in V position
Meter: 2/4, 4/4 or 6/8 (counted 123,123)
Jim Gold YouTube video: *https://www.youtube.com/watch?v=ofe23VmPsKk*
Introduction: 16 meas
Measures:

FIRST STEP
Moving Diag rt ctr and diag rt back
1   Step diag fwd on R (ct 1), step lft next to R (ct 2)
2   Fwd on R (ct 1-2)
3   Step fwd on L (ct 1-2)
4   Step diag back on R (ct 1),step lft next to R (ct 2)
5   Step back on R (ct 1-2)
6   Step back on L (ct 2)
Stamp and lift
7   Step R (ct 1), stamp L next to R (ct 2)
8   Step L (ct 1), lift R (ct 2)
Moving CW: 4 step grapevine, and 2 crosses to lft
9   Cross R front of L (ct 1),step L to lft (ct 2)
10   Step R behind L (ct 1). Step L to lft side (ct 2)
11   Cross R front of L (ct 1),step L to lft (ct 2)
12   Cross R front of L (ct 1), big "accented" lift L (ct 2)
Moving CCW: Two crosses to rt
13   Cross L over R (ct 1), step R to R (ct 2)
14   Cross L front of R (ct 1), lift R (ct 2)

SECOND STEP
Double Csardas break step
1   Step R to rt (ct 1). Close L to R (ct 2)
2   Step R to rt (ct 1). Tch L next to R (ct 2)
3   Step L to lft (ct 1), close R to L (ct 2)
4   Step L to lft (ct 1), tch R to L (ct 2)

ORDER OF STEPS
1. First Step: 2x; csardas break
2. First Step: 3x; add 1 csardas of meas 1 of "Double Csardas break step"
3. First Step: 2x; Csardas break
4. First Step: 2x

YADZHIISKATA (BULGARIA)

Dance Meaning: Unknown
Pronunciation: Yad zhis kata (Azh@ like As@ in measure)
Choreography: by Jim Gold in Bulgarian folk dance style
Music: Bulgarian Folklore Dances from the region of Veliko Turnovo. Using music
    from Bulgarian dance named AYadzhiiskata.@
Formation: Line. Hands in V positions (1 & 2), W position (3)
Meter: 2/4
Jim Gold YouTube video: https://www.youtube.com/watch?v=H45KXkTqGS8
Introduction: 8 measures
Measures:

FIRST STEP

Moving Rt (CCW), walk 4 steps. Hands in V (low hands) pos
1   L(ct 1), R(ct 2)
2   L(ct 1), R(ct 2)
Two back pas-de-bas 2-steps
3   Step fwd on L(ct 1), bring R behind L(ct &), step fwd on L(ct 2)
4   Step fwd on R(ct 1), bring L behind R(ct &), step fwd on R(ct 2)
      Walk 4 steps, one 2-step
5   L(ct 1), R(ct 2)
6   L(ct 1), R(ct 2)
7   Step fwd on L(ct 1), bring R behind L(ct &), step fwd on L(ct 2)
8   Face ctr, step on R(ct 1)
      Light stamp on L heel next to R(ct 2), raise hands to W pos

SECOND STEP

Into ctr (AAlunelul-like@ step)
1   Fall onto L ft(ct 1), stamp R no weight (ct &)
      fall onto R ft(ct 2), stamp L no weight (ct &)
2   fall onto L ft(ct 1), stamp R (ct &), stamp R again (ct 2)
      Out of ctr
3   R(ct 1), L(ct 2). Hands move slowly down to V pos (cts 1-2,1-2)
4   R(ct 1), light stamp on L heel next to R, no weight(ct 2), raise Hands
      to W pos
5-16   Repeat meas 1-4 3x

THIRD STEP

3 Lifts and 8-crossing steps. Hands in W pos
On lifts, bend body slightly and add slight twist to each lift
1   Step on L(ct 1), lift R(ct 2)
2   Step on R(ct 1), lift L(ct 2)

3	Step on R(ct 1), lift L(ct 2)
4	Cross R over L(ct 1), step on L in place(ct &)
	Step on R in place(ct 2)
	8-step cherkessia
5	Step on L in place(ct 1), cross R over L(ct &)
	Step on L in place(ct 2), step on R in place(ct &)
6	Cross L over R(ct 1), step on R in place(ct &)
	Step on L in place(ct 2), cross R over L(ct &)
7	Step on L(ct 1). Lift R(ct 2)
8	Step back on R(ct 1), step on L next to R(ct &)
	Step on R(ct 2)

ORDER OF STEPS:
1. First Step: 1x, Second Step: 4x, Third Step: 2x
2. First Step: 1x, Second Step: 4x, Third Step: 2x
3. First Step: 1x, Second Step: 4x, Third Step: 2x
4. First Step: 1x, Second Step: 4x, Third Step: 1x

YOM YOM NE PRISHYAL (Russia)

Dance Meaning: Why Didn't You Come
Pronunciation: Yom Yom Ne Prish-YAL
Choreography: By Jim Gold using traditional Russian steps
Music: "Maydan": Kazachiv Ensemble of Song and Dance
Formation: Open circle: Fists on hips Russian style
Meter: 4/4
Jim Gold YouTube Video:
>   1. **Teaching:** *https://www.youtube.com/watch?v=1bJv3vbJTjM*
>   2. **Monday Night dancers:** h*ttps://www.youtube.com/ watch?v=IWyRbP7Omkg*

Introduction: 8 measures
Measures:

FIRST STEP
>   **Proud Walk to the right, CCW**
1   R (ct 1), L (ct 2), step on R (ct 3)
>   Face forward, touch L forward (ct 4)
2   Step on L (ct 1), touch R forward (ct 2)
>   Step on R (ct 3), touch L forward (ct 4)
3-4   Repeat meas 1-2 in opp dir with opp ft
5   Repeat meas 1 while reach-spreading R hand and arm to right (ct 1-3)
>   Touch L ft forward, place R fist on R hip (ct 4)
6   Step on L (ct 1)
>   Place L fist on L hip, place R hand behind head, touch R ft forward (ct 2)
>   Step on R (ct 3)
>   Place R fist on R hip, place L hand behind head, touch L forward (ct 4)

SECOND STEP
>   **2 front pas de bas, fists on hips**
1   Step on L (ct 1), cross R over left (ct &), step on L in place (ct 2)
>   Step on R (ct 3), cross L over R (ct &), step on R in place (ct 4)
>   **4 push-steps moving to left, CW**
2   Weight on R, fall onto L ft, push R ft to right (ct 1), step on R next to L (ct &)
>   Weight on R, fall onto L ft, push R ft to right (ct 2), step on R next to L (ct &)
>   Weight on R, fall onto L ft, push R ft to right (ct 3), step on R next to L (ct &)
>   Fall onto L ft (ct 4), touch R ft next to L (ct &)

Slap and clap step

3   Standing with weight on L ft
Slap L side of hip with L hand (ct 1)
Raise R leg and slap above R knee (ct &)
Step on R (ct 2)
Clap both hands (ct 3)
Jump on both ft (ct 4)

4   Clap both hands in front of chest (ct 1)
Slap L thigh with R hand (ct &)
Clap both hand in front of chest (ct 2)
Slap R thigh with L hand (ct &)
Slap R thigh with R hand (ct 3)
Slap L thigh with L hand (ct &)
Clap both hands in front of chest (ct 4)

ZASHTEM (BULGARIA)

Dance Meaning: What do I have to live for?

Pronunciation: As written above Research: Martha Forsyth researched the title for me. See footnotes below .

Choreography: by Jim Gold in Bulgarian folk dance style

Music: Peya Za Vas: Rositsa Peicheva

Formation: Line. Holding hands in V position

Meter: 2/4

Jim Gold YouTube video: *https://www.youtube.com/watch?v=CuNBDf4UtP0*

Introduction: 14 Measures

Measures:

FIRST STEP

Face CCW (RLOD), hands down in V position
4 walking steps

1-2   Walk R (ct 1), L (ct 2), R (ct 1), L(ct 2)

        2 traveling two-steps

3-4   R (ct 1), L behind R (ct &), R (ct 2)
        L (ct 1), R behind R (ct &), L (ct 2)

5   Face ctr: Step R to rt (ct 1), step L behind R (ct 2)

        2 lifts

6   Step R to rt (ct 1), lift L (ct 2)

7   Step L in place (ct 1), lift R (ct 2)

8-12   Repeat meas 1-5

13   Step R to rt (ct 1), lift L (ct 2)

14   Step L in place (ct 1), lift R, hands move to W position (ct 2)

SECOND STEP

Hands remain in W position

1-7   Repeat First Step

        Grapevine (with dip) and lift

8   Step R to rt (ct 1)
        Step on L in front of R and dip on L (ct 2)

9   Step R to rt (ct 1), step L behind R (ct 2)

10   Step R to rt (ct 1), lift L (ct 2)

11   Step L in place (ct 1), lift R (ct 2)

        2 traveling "facing fwd" pas de bas

12   R (ct 1), step L behind R (ct &), R (ct 2)

13   L (ct 1), step R behind L (ct &), L (ct 2)

        Grapevine and lift

14   Step R to rt (ct 1), step L behind R (ct 2)

15   Step R to rt (ct 1), step L in front of R (ct 2)

16   Step R to rt (ct 1), lift L (ct 2)

17   Step L in place (ct 1), lift R (ct
18-33 Repeat meas 1-16
35   Step L to lft (ct 1), lift R and bring hands to V pos (ct 2)

ORDER OF STEPS
1. Step One: 3x, Step Two: 2x
2. Step One: 2x, Step 2: 2x
3. Step One: 2x, Step Two: 2x
4. Step One: 1x

From The Research Of Martha Forsyth

Listening to this, it sounded (esp. in the accompaniment), almost Serbian to me. "So I googled the title of the song. Found a very similar but quite different version —sung by Tincho Sevdalinov and the Vievska Folk Group! *This* one sounds unmistakeably Rhodope to me! The notes have a "glossary", but it's dialect in Bulgarian:

> *http://vbox7.com/play:ce6acbec,* and also
> *http://vbox7.com/play:2cb0a7d0&al=2&vid=7851517*

Be forewarned: vbox is *very* slow to load! best to pause it till it's all loaded and then play.

"Very interesting: I told you "Zashtim" is "not Bulgarian"? I couldn't find it in ANY of my Bg dialect (or non-dialect) source books. But the place I found it was....in a *Russian* dictionary from the 1860s!

"And also I found that the film with which the Tincho Sevdalinov version is associated is based on a short story by Nikolaj Haitov.

"I guess this is why I'm so welcoming to such questions. . .I never know where they'll lead me.

"Anyway here's your text and translation (this is from the Sevdalinov version, I didn't take the time to compare it to Rositsa's):"

> *What do I have to live for*
> *in this lying world,*
> *lying and sinful?*
>
> *When I don't have a horse to ride*
> *when I don't have a home to sit in*
> *when I don't have a love to love.*

I had one love
and she got married yesterday.
I liked another
and she got engaged last night.

Tell me, mother, tell me
what I have to live for
in this life?

ZELENA GORA (BULGARIA)

Dance Meaning: Green Forest
Pronunciation: Zelena Gora
Choreography: by Jim Gold in Bulgarian folk dance style.
Music: Linden Group from Blagoevgrad
Formation: Open circle, hands in W position
Meter: 7/8: slow/quick/quick: s, q, q
Jim Gold YouTube video: *https://www.youtube.com/watch?v=K__AoWMDzaw*
Introduction: 8 measures
Measures:

FIRST STEP
4 measure Lesnoto
1   Face ctr: Step R to rt (s), lift L (q), step L over R (q)
2   Repeat meas 1
3   Step R to rt (s), lift L (q q)
4   Step on L (s), lift R (q q)
5   Step R to rt (s), step L behind R (q), step R to rt (q)
Face CCW
6   Step on L (s), step R (q), step L (q)
7   Fact ctr: Repeat meas 3-4

SECOND STEP
Walking and pas de pas, face CCW
1   Step fwd on R (s), fwd on L (q), fwd on R (q)
2   Repeat meas 1 opp ft
Face ctr
3   Step on R (s), cross L over R (q), step on R in place (q)
4   Repeat meas 3 opp ft, opp dir

ORDER OF STEPS
1. First Step: 2x, Second Step: 2x

CPSIA information can be obtained
at www.ICGtesting.com
Printed in the USA
JSHW020744040120
3344JS00001BB/1